INVESTING IN
JUSTICE

An Introduction to Legal Finance, Lawsuit
Advances and Litigation Funding

———⟨○⟩———

MAX VOLSKY, ESQ.

The Legal Finance Journal
The Standard for the Legal Finance Industry

Published by
The Legal Finance Journal
130 West Pleasant Avenue, Suite 279
Maywood, New Jersey 07607
www.legalfinancejournal.com
info@legalfinancejournal.com

ISBN: 978-0-9885105-0-0

Edited by: Nathaniel T. Noda

Cover and interior design by Kate Irwin

"Man's mind, once stretched by a new idea,
never regains its original dimensions."

Oliver Wendell Holmes, Jr.
Associate Justice of the
U.S. Supreme Court, 1902–1932

TABLE OF CONTENTS

PREFACE

The scarcity of money leads to considerable distortions in our society that can affect us profoundly. Undeniably, those with financial means will often enjoy disproportionate access to many of the basic rights that ought to be available without regard to income or wealth. Perhaps one of the starkest examples of this disparity is evident in our legal system, which requires its participant to have abundant capital to access justice. As an attorney, I have seen firsthand the enormous challenges plaintiffs face as they contend with professional defendants armed with considerable resources, and no compunction toward exploiting those resources to outlast and intimidate their opponents.

In the late nineties, I became involved in the formation of a new industry—called legal finance—then a still largely unfamiliar class of financial products that promised to balance these inequities by allowing plaintiffs to sell a participation right in their legal claims to investors before they were resolved. Legal finance created a new asset that could be monetized by plaintiffs to receive capital, which could be used to improve their chances of success in their litigation. Since then, I have invested in the outcome of lawsuits by providing capital to thousands of personal injury and commercial plaintiffs across North America. As one of the first participants in this field, I have witnessed the development of this industry from its humble beginnings to one of the most promising alternative asset classes in the world.

The legal finance industry arose as a market response to the challenge faced by millions of litigants who struggle every day to achieve favorable outcomes in their lawsuits against opponents who can—and most often do—greatly outspend them. By providing funding to these disenfranchised plaintiffs, the nascent legal finance industry has leveled the legal playing field for countless individuals and companies who otherwise would have nowhere to turn.

Systemic economic changes are contributing to a rapid expansion of this field by driving demand for lawsuit-linked products. The 2008 financial crisis has significantly eroded personal wealth, while also impacting businesses and organizations of all sizes, making them less capable of financing the costs of protracted litigation. Individuals, companies, municipalities, schools, and non-profit organizations have all experienced liquidity constraints, which have similarly impeded their access to justice.

As this industry continues to mature—expanding the number of products and markets across the world—it has worn away at the historical inequities that have long marginalized litigants and distorted outcomes. Much as recent advancements have shaped information technology, medicine, and other sectors undergoing rapid transformation, the emergence of innovative tools like legal finance means that the funding of dispute resolution will never be the same.

Every cycle of progress, however, can induce a wave of discontent from those who stand to lose the most from increased transparency, efficiency, and ease of access. New industries must often battle against the overzealous disparagement leveled against them by those who have a stake in preserving the status quo. In a bid to preserve their dominance, opponents can and often will use everything in their power to obscure the benefits of new paradigms by injecting controversy into conversations about their adoption.

Legal finance is no exception.

As the debate rages about the desirability of this practice, markets have yet to fully embrace legal finance as a solution to the imbalances of the justice system. In the United States more than anywhere else, this debate has been clouded by legal anachronisms and blind formalism that have engendered a perception of uncertainty about the industry's legality. As a result of the debate ignoring the truly important social function of this new and vital resource, most litigants continue to struggle within the confines of a legal system that is inherently stacked against them.

Clearly, the legal finance naysayers are behind the curve of a global trend poised to significantly change the way disputes are financed in the future. Like all forms of innovation, however, legal finance has inherently resisted all attempts at suppression; it grows ever more in popularity and will continue to do so until a tipping point is reached.

Yet even as this emerging asset class attracts greater attention from consumers, investors, and policy makers alike, the public's basic understanding of legal finance remains largely superficial. This book is an outgrowth of the lack of comprehensive and reliable industry information—or even appropriate terminology—to describe this sector's core products and services. It is intended as a resource for investors, consumers, the legal community, policymakers, business executives and academia to better understand the history and development of the legal finance marketplace. It strives to provide a comprehensive overview of third-party legal finance in the United States (with a discussion of the Australian and United Kingdom's industries as well), with an eye toward analyzing the emerging opportunities from my unique perspective as one of the first participants in this field. This book also endeavors to help investors make better funding decisions by providing a contextual framework for the industry, including:

- establishing the investment case for this business;

- defining the most common features of its products;
- describing the investment process;
- identifying and responding to criticism of legal finance;
- examining the regulation of this industry; and
- charting the course of evolution for this growing field.

Like many burgeoning industries, a small group of farseeing leaders have embraced legal finance and established the first building blocks of a sector that is redefining old notions of dispute resolution, both in North America and around the world. Through their efforts, capital markets are now beginning to understand the industry's potential, and a growing list of institutional investors are expanding their presence in this market.

This book is dedicated to the pioneers of the legal finance field who, through their vision and fortitude, have created a platform that is transforming an obsolete and improvident system into a fairer and more balanced one for millions of litigants worldwide. I hope this book will aid them in their efforts as they continue to refine and improve their business models to provide greater judicial access for all.

CHAPTER I
LEGAL FINANCE OVERVIEW

> "Equal justice under law is not merely a caption on the facade of the Supreme Court building; it is perhaps the most inspiring ideal of our society. It is one of the ends for which our entire legal system exists ... it is fundamental that justice should be the same, in substance and availability, without regard to economic status."
>
> *– Lewis Powell, Jr., U.S. Supreme Court Justice (ret.), during his tenure as president of the American Bar Association*

Access to Justice and Litigation Costs

Each day, people are hurt by circumstances beyond their control. These "Slings and Arrows of outrageous Fortune," as William Shakespeare's *Hamlet* described them, wound bodies, hearts, and purse strings alike. While the legal system was designed and intended to provide a means to redress those injuries, the harsh financial realities entailed by that system often prevent some of the most worthy of claimants from even seeking—much less obtaining—legal relief. The four stories that follow illustrate the wide range of contexts in which such overwhelming financial burdens can prevent injured parties from receiving the remedies they deserve.

●●●

Tim and his wife Caroline suffer a serious car accident. Both are severely injured and taken to the emergency room. After several surgeries, Tim is confined to a wheelchair and will be unable to walk for more than a year. Caroline suffers a concussion and numerous fractures. She will need to stay home for at least three months.

Unable to work, Tim is fired from his job as a sales clerk while his wife takes unpaid medical leave from her job as a bookkeeper. Like many Americans, Tim's family is uninsured and has neither a safety net nor emergency funds. The couple is already two months behind on their mortgage and other bills have started to pile up. They have two small children.

Tim's friend refers him to a personal injury lawyer who informs him that he has an excellent case, but also cautions that it will take a year or more to receive any money from the insurance company. Tim and Caroline will eventually get back on their feet—all they need is a lifeline to help pay bills until they recover from the trauma of the accident. Given their precarious situation, they also know that if the insurance company offers them any money now—even an amount far less than the case is worth—they will probably accept it. As far as they know, they have no other choice.

●●●

Susan is general counsel at a company that manufactures remodeling solutions for expensive homes. A weak housing market means that sales are poor, and the company now struggles to finance its operations. Susan's company is trying to branch into more profitable lines of business, but cash is always a problem. Last year, one of its suppliers, a large titanium producer, shipped defective tracking wheels that were ultimately used by the company in products it sold to its customers, causing Susan's firm to lose significant market share.

Susan knows she has a strong case against the titanium company, a case which is potentially worth tens of millions for her company. But she also knows bringing suit will be very expensive. She understands that her company's management has always perceived the legal department as a cost center—necessary to put out fires and help the company navigate the laws applicable to its industry—not as a potential generator of revenue. To make matters worse, there is simply not enough cash on hand to engage in a speculative lawsuit that could end up costing millions. Susan needs another stakeholder in the outcome of her case because her company cannot afford to bring the lawsuit. Unless someone commits to paying all the expenses— and perhaps even advances the company funds for working capital—her firm will have to forfeit this valuable opportunity.

• • •

Jonathan is a young inventor who spent several years developing a process that allows electronic devices to communicate at long distances. He is surprised to learn that a Fortune 500 company just entered the market with the very idea he patented almost a year ago. After consulting with an attorney, he learned that the company is infringing on his patent and may be liable to him for up to $100 million for their actions. Jon's lawyer also informed him that the average patent infringement case costs $3 million or more to prosecute.

Jon's invention has been misappropriated by a corporate giant with abundant resources to defend any lawsuit. Faced with the daunting prospect of spending millions of dollars—money he does not have—the young inventor is effectively denied any meaningful access to the justice system to redress the harm he has suffered. His only hope is to find a third-party investor to pay for the costs of the lawsuit.

• • •

Anne and David are managing partners of a medium-sized law firm that represents low-income mothers against hospitals whose negligence during delivery caused severe birth defects in their children. Those defects will develop into serious illnesses requiring expensive full-time care for the rest of their children's lives.

Anne and David's firm has the only lawyers in the state who specialize in these complex and expensive cases. They finance all the costs of these lawsuits themselves by taking each case on contingency—an arrangement where plaintiffs do not pay unless they win their cases. Their office has ten more cases just like this one, and each lawsuit costs over $1 million to prosecute and lasts an average of three years.

As they develop each case for trial, the costs often prove unpredictable. The law firm needs to hire additional paralegals to help with a major case involving brain damage, a claim potentially worth millions. The expert witness fees for this case will also be double what they originally projected. Even time is a rarefied and costly commodity, as most of their cases take far longer to resolve due to bottlenecks in their state's court system. Without an immediate capital infusion, Anne and David may not be able to properly litigate their biggest cases. In fact, they can hardly keep their firm afloat, putting at peril not only each and every case they are handling, but also the futures of the disabled children they represent.

If Anne and David go out of business, children with birth defects in their state will lose their only champion, and many people will lose their jobs. Anne and David applied for a bank loan, but were rejected because their financials were complicated and most of their collateral was tied up in complex intangibles—assets that banks often do not understand. The partners know there is significant value in their cases, if only someone were prepared to properly evaluate and monetize that risk.

• • •

Situations like these happen every day. Despite our best efforts, the United States remains a country of great inequities, where many basic rights of an advanced society are accessible only to those who can afford it. This is evident in healthcare and education, where outcomes are sharply divided along socioeconomic lines. It is also evident in our legal system, which is not immune to distortions created by mismatches of capital. Our complex and often expensive legal system has been historically starved of capital, creating a pressing need for new finance options to help increase access to the legal system and reduce the adverse effects of unforeseen events.

In much of the world, and the United States in particular, access to justice depends on money. Litigation invariably is an expensive proposition. Many factors contribute to the cost of litigation: attorney fees for discovery, research, depositions, interrogatories, motions, conferences, witness preparation, trials, subpoenas, appeals, as well as expenses associated with court fees, consultants, and investigations. These costs will also increase if the legal battle occurs in comparatively expensive jurisdictions like New York or Los Angeles.

Depositions can cost from $1,000 to $5,000 per day, excluding the cost of pre-interviewing potential witnesses and other parties to the case. Expert witnesses and their opinions can run from several thousand to hundreds of thousands of dollars, depending on their hourly rate and how much time each expert must devote to studying the facts of the case and developing useful testimony. A court reporter can charge as much as $1,000 per day, with additional fees applicable for a videographer to be present.[1] An attorney's time is a separate matter, with most lawyers charging a steep hourly fee. If the case is appealed, these expenses can easily double. For more complex cases, travel expenses, document management and production costs also add up. Worse yet, all of these expenses do not even account for the time spent in-house by corporate counsel and employees supporting the litigation. Executives of Fortune 500 companies expend approximately 20 percent of their time working on litigation related issues.[2]

Some estimates put the average cost of a civil lawsuit in the United States as high as $50,000. In a system where money serves as a gatekeeper to justice, the explosion of litigation costs in recent years has only worsened the disparities between those who can and cannot afford the steep price tag. As the stakes rise, litigation costs also escalate dramatically. The monumental costs of litigation have affected even the system's largest and wealthiest participants. The eLaw Forum has estimated that Fortune 500 companies spent approximately $210 billion on litigation related expenses in 2006, roughly one-third of their after-tax profits and 28 times their CEO compensation.[3]

The Conference on Civil Litigation conducted a 2010 survey of Fortune 200 companies about their long-term litigation cost trends. The survey confirmed empirically what corporate counsel had known anecdotally: the transaction costs of litigating against large companies are so exorbitant that they exceed the amount at issue in all but the largest cases.[4]

Litigation transaction costs, excluding amounts of judgments and settlements, have risen substantially over the past few years, both on average and as a percent of corporate revenue. For example, the average outside litigation cost per reporting company was nearly $115 million in 2008, up 73 percent from $66 million in 2000, representing an average annual increase of nine percent.[5] Between 2000 and 2008, average annual litigation costs as a percent of revenues increased 78 percent for the 14 companies that provided this data.[6]

Patent litigation reveals a similar problem. In 2010, 2,892 patent infringement actions were filed in the United States—many with multiple defendants.[7] The American Intellectual Property Law Association's 2011 Economic Survey reports that the median litigation costs per party for a patent infringement lawsuit when less than $1 million is at risk is $490,000 through the end of discovery and $916,000 through trial; when $1 million to $25 million is at risk, costs per party rises to $1.6 million through the end of discovery and $2.8 million through trial. Costs per party can skyrocket to an average of $3.6 million through the end of discovery and $6 million through trial when more than $25 million is at stake.[8]

The U.S. legal system imposes a much greater cost burden on companies than systems found in most other countries. As a percent of revenue, companies spend a disproportionate amount on litigation in the United States relative to their expenditures in foreign jurisdictions. In fact, as a percent of revenue, relative U.S. costs are four to nine times higher than those in non-U.S. systems.[9]

To a large extent, the high cost of bringing a lawsuit in common law jurisdictions is due to their overwhelming complexity. Common-law jurisdictions operate as an adversarial system where the inquisitory process is directed by the litigants themselves, rather than the inquisitor judge found in civil law systems. In common-law countries like the United States, Canada, United Kingdom, and Australia, the skill and resources of the attorney, as well as the defendant's ability to outlast opponents, greatly impacts the outcomes of disputes.

The United States' situation in particular is even more complex. Extensive discovery rules and the availability of adjudication by jury make it a particularly onerous and expensive jurisdiction for litigation. The need for a well-prepared, talented and motivated attorney is therefore paramount.

A significant portion of litigation expenses arise in the context of discovery. Discovery is a pre-trial phase of a lawsuit in which each party obtains evidence from the opposing party. It is conducted by means of devices like interrogatories (questions and answers written under oath), requests for production of documents, requests for admissions and depositions of the parties. The discovery of information is crucial to any lawsuit, and parties may battle to gain information, to conceal information, and to present information in a way that better persuades judges, juries, and opponents to accept their interpretation of the law. Much of the fighting between litigants often takes place during the discovery period.

Extensive discovery rules are a part of the adversarial process in the United States, allowing the parties a great deal of latitude to produce evidence, frequently creating a glut of documents and information. This glut has been made even more ponderous by the rise of e-discovery, which contrary to expectations has dramatically increased the volume of information for a typical case.

For example, the ratio of pages discovered to pages entered as exhibits is as high as a thousand to one. In 2008, on average, 4,980,441 pages of documents were produced in discovery in major cases that went to trial, but only 4,772 of those pages actually were marked into evidence.[10] For the period 2006–2008, the average company that participated in the cost survey paid mean discovery costs per case of $621,880 to $2,993,567.[11] Companies at the top of the scale paid mean costs ranging from $2,354,868 to $9,759,900.[12]

As a result of this complexity, the United States has fallen behind other developed countries in terms of access to justice for non-tort related claims. The 2012 World Justice Project's "Rule of Law Index" ranked the United States 22nd, below Estonia and Botswana in access to and affordability of legal counsel in civil disputes.[13]

The United States also consistently lags behind other developed countries in terms of investment in affordable legal services as a percentage of gross national product, or GNP.[14] There is neither a constitutional nor statutory right in the U.S. to receive the assistance of appointed counsel in civil cases, except perhaps the narrow practice adopted by some states relating to parental rights. For example, 81 percent of low-income Americans do not use legal assistance because they cannot afford the high fees.[15] Similarly, millions of New Yorkers with civil legal problems cannot afford an attorney. In a 2010 New York study, it was shown that 95 percent of people who appear in housing court are unrepresented.

The same is true in consumer credit matters, where 44 percent of people in foreclosures represent themselves—typically against well-represented financial institutions.[16]

Many poor and middle-class New Yorkers lack access to the courts for eviction disputes, mortgage matters, and even simple disputes like credit card fraud. In fact, they are precluded from meaningful participation in any civil matter that lies outside the competence of small claims courts—usually when the amount in dispute is above $5,000.

In personal injury cases, plaintiffs also experience financial problems that impact their claims. While meritorious cases will readily attract good counsel willing to represent their clients on a contingency basis, plaintiffs frequently find themselves unable to support themselves and their families after an accident and during the pendency of the claim. Because Americans generally have inadequate safety nets, their financial situation frequently becomes precarious as their ability to work is impacted by injury.

Financial asymmetry, therefore, provides well-funded defendants with an overly potent defensive weapon. In patent infringement cases, for example, defendants have long exploited the financial weaknesses of plaintiffs, engaging in a costly war of attrition intended to exhaust and overwhelm.[17] Unrepentant defendants in personal injury matters often pursue a similar strategy.[18]

As the human and financial costs for marshaling a case tend to increase, many individuals and companies who feel they have a compelling case will choose to defer or ultimately abandon legal recourse. In commercial cases, many potential litigants who seek justice are unable to pursue their claim due to the high costs associated with lawsuits and the uncertainty that accompanies each claim. They are forced to conclude that the cost of pursuing their case in court is too high when considering the various possible outcomes, especially if their opponent is a wealthy defendant with ready access to legal representation. In personal injury claims, plaintiffs are also at a disadvantage. With most cases lasting a year or more, plaintiffs desperate for money often feel pressure to settle much sooner and for far less than their injuries would otherwise deserve. In all types of litigation, even when the underlying case is quite promising, many decide not to sue, or to settle for a fraction of what their cases are worth.

Although the attorney's contingent fee has gained ground in equalizing access to justice for tort cases, it does not go far enough to help plaintiffs with living expenses. It is also not widely available for cases that are not tort related. Other common-law countries that utilize a loser-pays system have to contend with the fee-shifting requirements imposed by the English rule, which further discourage plaintiffs from taking risk considering the possibility of having to pay their opponents' defense costs.

Accordingly, a great imbalance of resources exists between average and wealthy litigants, not only creating impediments to judicial access but a distortion of legal outcomes for the undercapitalized. This problem is exacerbated in situations where one party is a repeat player and the other is a one-time participant.[19] The one-time litigant will be more cautious of proceeding to trial, more risk-averse and perhaps eager to settle. As a result, they are generally in a weaker bargaining position, and compelled to accept settlements that do not reflect the underlying merits of their claims.[20]

Faced with the prospect of forfeiting their chance to redress their grievances, individuals and companies need a stakeholder in the outcome of litigation—a "law banker" to help plaintiffs monetize the outcome of their claims so they can afford the high costs of litigation. Without the ability to harness this value, plaintiffs are either forced to accept worse outcomes or completely denied access to justice.

Many believe that lawsuit investors can level the playing field for litigants by creating a more efficient and equitable means of redistributing risk. Third-party legal finance has the capacity to equalize the bargaining power of litigants by providing funding to undercapitalized plaintiffs through the use of novel financial products.

What is Legal Finance?

At its most basic level, "legal finance" is the practice where a third party unrelated to the subject matter of a lawsuit provides money to a party involved in litigation to help further that party's objectives in the legal claim in return for a financial reward. The capital provided by lawsuit investors may help plaintiffs pay for living expenses or directly pay for some of the costs of litigation, including attorneys' fees, expert witness fees, court costs, and other expenses associated with a lawsuit. Capital from a legal finance provider may be used to fund operating expenses for companies involved in litigation. It can also be provided directly to law firms to finance their operations. The financial reward for making the investment can take different forms, including a flat fee, a multiple of the amount advanced, a percentage of the amount recovered, an interest rate when it is a loan to a law firm, or some other basis of compensation.

The History and Evolution of Legal Finance

In the United States, various forms of third-party lawsuit investing have endured for many years. For example, patent investing is practiced by some of the world's largest financial institutions, which through subsidiaries acquire rights to certain valuable patents and enforce those rights by filing patent infringement lawsuits against anyone who uses commercially similar technology without paying royalties.

Patents are regularly monetized and sold in the context of bankruptcy. Public policy favors such deals, and federal law specifically authorizes transfers.[21] A market for judgments has also existed for many years, allowing financial institutions like credit card companies and commercial lenders to regularly engage in the sale and transfer of judgments against their debtors.

Investors have for a long time made bets on lawsuits. Some have acquired or sold short stocks in publicly traded companies that are parties to lawsuits with the expectation that their stock price of will either go up or down, depending on the company's fortunes in the lawsuit. In two recent examples, both the pharmaceutical giant Merck and Canada's Research in Motion (RIM) had to contend with significant changes to their market capitalization as a result of legal events relating to their core products.[22] Shares of HTC and Bank of America also experienced significant volatility as a result of lawsuits relating to their businesses.[23]

Merck was besieged by a wave of litigation arising from its failed Vioxx drug, which the company removed from the market amid allegations of an increased rate of cardiovascular problems in patients. After the drug's withdrawal announcement, Merck's share price fell nearly thirty percent. Similarly, investors had an opportunity to capitalize on litigation events relating to RIM's BlackBerry patent lawsuit by speculating on the company's share price based on their evolving expectations regarding the outcome of that lawsuit.

Many other examples of legal finance have emerged throughout the years. The direct financing of lawsuits by a third party was first permitted in the 1960s for civil rights litigation supported by the NAACP, where the practice was permitted so long as the funding organization did not control the litigation.[24] In 1976, Carl E. Person—who would later become a 2010 candidate for New York State attorney general and a 2012 Libertarian Party candidate for president—tried and failed to raise an antitrust litigation fund by offering shares of stock to investors.[25] Waterbed inventor Charles P. Hall's efforts to commercialize his concept failed, and by 1985 a number of knock-off manufacturers were squeezing him out of the market. Hall sued the infringing manufacturers using a war chest of $750,000 given by his investors to sue those manufacturers that were infringing on his patents. His efforts were finally vindicated in 1991 when a court awarded him $6.8 million in damages.[26]

Another example arose from the 1980s savings and loan debacle. More than 120 breach-of-contract suits were filed against the federal government by savings institutions seeking restitution and damages related to the dissolution of the Federal Home Loan Bank Board. In that securitization, a number of savings and loan companies sold shares that were linked to this federal litigation. These shares were listed on NASDAQ and traded under various names including litigation tracking warrants, contingent payment rights, and contingent litigation recovery participation interests.[27]

Historical Prohibition: A Legacy of Medieval Times

Direct forms of legal finance, particularly the funding of lawsuit expenses by repeat players who are unrelated to the subject matter of a dispute, have emerged as an asset class only recently. This is due to a degree of legal uncertainty that has for years discouraged investment in this area. In fact, three medieval English doctrines—"maintenance," "champerty," and "barratry"—historically prohibited third-party financing of lawsuits in the United States and most other common law countries. Maintenance involves an arrangement where a party supports another to enable him or her to further a claim. Champerty is a specific form of maintenance, where an unrelated party strikes a bargain with a litigant to financially support the litigation in return for a share of the proceeds from that claim. Finally, barratry entails the encouragement of another to bring or continue a claim. In its *In re Primus* opinion, the United States Supreme Court drew clearer distinctions between the three doctrines: "Put simply, maintenance is helping another prosecute a suit; champerty is maintaining a suit in return for a financial interest in the outcome; and barratry is a continuing practice of maintenance or champerty."[28]

In medieval England, maintenance and champerty provoked ligation by the powerful as a means of settling scores. Feudal lords and other privileged members of society would often assist others, usually those of little means, by supporting their legal disputes against a third party, who was often the underwriter's personal or political enemy. Champerty in particular became a means by which powerful men increased their influence by waging a private war through the courts. There are three elements to champerty: (1) an unrelated party undertakes; (2) to further another's legal claim; (3) in return for a portion of any favorable outcome.[29]

Like any strategic tool, champerty can be invaluable when used appropriately and damaging when exploited. Responding to concerns regarding overzealous and one-sided champerty, English law in most jurisdictions came to prohibit such arrangements. Thereafter, most colonies that imported their laws from England —including many U.S. states—passed laws designed to protect litigants from "officious intermeddling" and profiteering from the sale of legal claims to third parties. These doctrines reflected a public policy that sought to discourage frivolous litigation, quarrels, resistance to settlement, and interference with the attorney-client relationship. The prevailing view was that litigation—even involving meritorious claims—should be inherently discouraged.

Over time, as other means of controlling abuses of the legal system became more effective, the need for the prohibitions on champerty, maintenance and barratry receded. As parties in civil litigation are responsible for their own legal costs, the American civil justice system increasingly recognized that access to justice depends upon the broad availability of legal representation for all socioeconomic levels. The public policy for increasing access to the legal system for those that could least afford it overrode the concerns underlying the prohibition policies in many states. Today, widespread exceptions to the champerty doctrine recognize that financial considerations often influence access to justice. One of the most prominent exceptions to champerty is the attorney's contingent fee.

An Exception Arises: The Contingent Fee

From very early in the United States' history, Americans seeking monetary damages have retained lawyers on a contingency basis, which means that the attorney is paid only if there is a favorable judgment or settlement. While legislation authorizing similar "no win, no fee" agreements in other countries is a relatively new development, the United States has used contingent fee arrangements for more than a century.

Americans have traditionally purchased the services of attorneys in one of three ways. First, a client and attorney might agree upon a *fixed fee* for a specified service—generally for common and predictable legal services like wills or real estate transactions. Second, an attorney may charge an *hourly fee* for more complex assignments, including preparing contracts, giving tax advice, or engaging in commercial litigation for monetary damages. Third, a client and attorney may enter into a *contingent fee arrangement* where the client will pay their attorney a fixed percentage of a recovery in a lawsuit—typically a third, but in some cases up to 50 percent of the recovery.

Widely regarded as a vital tool for poor and middle income people to gain access to the justice system, the contingent fee has been uniformly adopted by all fifty states. It remains the most common form of third-party legal finance, and is currently utilized by most personal injury attorneys in the United States as well as a growing number of practitioners in other countries.

Some historians trace these types of arrangements to the time of the American Revolution. Thereafter, the practice became more engrained within the legal culture through the experience of settlers in the American frontier.[30] The development and pervasive adoption of the contingent fee in the United States was a response to unique conditions integral to the American experience in the nineteenth century.

At the time, contingent fees were often pursued where the plaintiff had a just cause but no money on hand to pursue it. Many settlers purchased their titles from squatter-enclosers and built homes, cleared farms and paid taxes for years on these properties.[31] Due to problems with their title, they were subject to ejection by richer developers claiming ownership over the same land. As many dispossessed frontier settlers lacked the money needed to pursue their legal claims, the contingent fee emerged as a way to help them gain access to the courts.[32]

The Ohio Supreme Court, in *Key v. Vattier*, famously recognized that a poor individual, "placed in the power of unfeeling and rapacious men, is illegally and oppressively stripped of his property, and turned, with his family, destitute, desolate."[33] By the time of the *Vattier* opinion in 1824, the contingent fee had already become a popular and ubiquitous payment mechanism for people of all dispositions. Contingency clients included merchants and creditors, heirs of millionaires, U.S. diplomats, and several Indian tribes.[34] Lawyers utilizing contingency arrangements included such accomplished counsel as Henry Clay and Daniel Webster.[35] Following the Civil War, clients retained lawyers on a contingency basis in a wide variety of disputes, including shareholder suits against corporations, depositor suits against banks, claims against railroads, and claims against the government.

The contingent fee became even more widespread through the rapid economic transformation heralded by the Industrial Revolution of the late nineteenth century. At the time, the struggle between labor and capital, especially in the booming manufacturing sector, created new personal injury claims that could not be adequately addressed by existing negligence arrangements, all of which required plaintiffs to have substantial resources to hire a lawyer. This occurred in an environment where thousands of aggressive first- and second-generation Americans were breaking into the legal industry—a parochial profession that was openly hostile to them. As a result of discrimination within their own guild, they further popularized the new payment mechanism to help attract clients, which allowed low-income workers to redress the difficult working conditions that existed during that period.

While some contingent arrangements were challenged in court, virtually all were deemed to be valid and binding. In 1908, the American Bar Association (ABA) finally endorsed contingent fees, and by 1965 the practice had been adopted in all states. As a result, an important exception was carved out of the champerty doctrine—one that set the stage for the continued erosion of prohibitions against legal finance.

In addition to the doctrines of maintenance, champerty and barratry, other factors also complicate third-party investing in lawsuits. Because investing in lawsuits is generally a high-risk bet, investors are often compelled to demand high returns for their capital. Legal finance transactions, however, are sometimes mistaken for loans due to their novel characteristics. For this reason, the flow of capital in this space was discouraged by state laws against usury, or the lending of money at high interest rates.

Usury: A Lingering Specter

Usury is the practice of charging excessive or illegal interest rates on loans. Prohibitions on usury have existed for thousands of years, sometimes as a result of religious or moral beliefs. Islam, for example, has very strict prohibitions against the charging of interest on loans. Governments in many countries have historically enacted usury laws to discourage unscrupulous lenders from taking advantage of unsophisticated borrowers. In the United States, many states have also enacted usury laws—some dating back to the colonial period—to protect consumers from overzealous creditors.

Concerned that usury laws had begun to undermine economic growth and efficiency, England and a number of U.S. states repealed their usury statutes in the mid to late nineteenth century. By the early twentieth century, however, many U.S. states had reinstated prohibitions on usury because of concerns over predatory lending. Today, most states maintain laws regulating the maximum interest rate on loans, though many of those laws exempt certain large transactions and corporations—allowing some to borrow at higher rates than usury statutes usually permit.

In most states, the elements of usury are: (1) an agreement to lend money; (2) the borrower's absolute obligation to repay the loan; (3) a greater compensation for making the loan than is allowed by the state's usury statute; and (4) an intention to take more money for the loan than the law allows.[36]

As a general matter, courts do not favor a finding of usury and the burden of proof is on the party asserting it. Nevertheless, a loan that requires an absolute obligation to pay interest that violates the state's usury statute is technically illegal as a matter of law. This has discouraged any meaningful investment in lawsuits until the advent of a new product: the non-recourse lawsuit advance for tort claims.

The Birth of Lawsuit Advances for Tort Claims

The origins of the legal finance industry in the United States can be traced to a company called Plaintiff Support Services. In 1992, personal injury lawyer (and thereafter the founder of law firm lender Counsel Financial) Joseph DiNardo faced a problem common to many attorneys: his clients needed money for living expenses while their cases were pending but his firm was ethically prohibited from funding their living expenses. After his search for a legal finance company turned up empty, he encouraged mortgage banker Ken Polowitz to start a firm called Plaintiff Support

Services in Buffalo, New York, to provide cash advances for living expenses to plaintiffs involved in tort lawsuits.[37] DiNardo recognized a demand for capital to fund living expenses from injured plaintiffs who were not being served by traditional financial institutions.

The company most often credited with popularizing the industry, though, is Future Settlement Funding. In 1994, after a fortuitous investment in his housekeeper's lawsuit spawned a business idea, Perry Walton, a Nevada businessman with a checkered past, established a funding company. Walton realized that millions of other people involved in tort lawsuits were similarly situated—they were in need of money to sustain themselves but without any collateral or borrowing power. Walton began investing in claims by offering plaintiffs cash advances in return for a fee if the case was won in court or settled. His company charged a simple monthly interest of 15 percent or a repayment multiple of three times the investment. The longer the underlying claim remained unresolved, the greater the plaintiff's repayment obligation would become.

After partnering with a marketing expert, Walton began conducting training seminars in Las Vegas for people interested in opening similar businesses who would become brokers for his company. He claims to have taught about 600 students. Within a short time, Walton's graduates expanded the availability of lawsuit advances as many small companies entered the field to create a cottage industry. Although a trail of unfortunate investment decisions and negative case precedent ultimately bankrupted Walton's company, his legacy in creating a new industry has endured.

The new lawsuit-linked financial product pioneered by Polowitz and Walton came at a time when courts already viewed the doctrines of champerty, maintenance, and barratry as mostly antiquated and obsolete. In 1997, the Supreme Judicial Court of Massachusetts held in *Saladini v. Righellis* that the common law prohibition against champerty was void in Massachusetts.[38] Similarly, an Arizona court of appeals held that champerty did not apply in that state. Other states, like New Jersey, have never prohibited champerty. With most of the cases supporting the prohibition of champerty having been decided more than one hundred years ago, many states refused to void contracts based on an outdated doctrine.

At the same time, lawsuit advances do not have the features of traditional loans and therefore lie outside the definition of most states' usury statutes. Lawsuit advances are non-recourse, which is a no-win, no-fee arrangement similar to a contingent fee. For a financing transaction to be usurious, it must have the most important feature of a loan: it must create an absolute obligation on the part of the recipient to repay it without regard to any circumstances that may excuse such repayment. If an obligation is contingently repayable and not absolute—such as the obligation commonly found in lawsuit advances—there can be no usury, though courts have generally required that the likelihood of losing the case be substantial and not too remote.

The Next Wave: Direct Legal Finance

The advent of the lawsuit cash advance for tort claims was a boon to other lawsuit-linked products. In 2001, several companies trailblazing the lawsuit advance market began offering contingency law firms various specialty debt products through their subsidiaries, products secured by the firms' fees from tort cases. Some companies had also invested in the outcomes of commercial lawsuits on a limited basis by providing funding directly to plaintiff companies.

In 2007, the U.S. legal finance industry witnessed another milestone when the U.K.-based Juridica Investments Limited floated its shares on London Stock Exchange's Alternative

Investment Market. Juridica specializes in direct financing of commercial claims—paying the expenses associated with bringing a lawsuit to resolution and sharing in the proceeds, primarily in the United States. Over the next three years, Juridica deployed more than $157 million in 23 cases, making it one of the most important players in legal finance market today. Within two years, other companies—public and private—followed suit. One of them, Burford Capital, floated their shares in London in 2009, becoming the second U.K.-based public company to specialize in funding commercial lawsuits in the United States.

The State of Legal Finance Today

Legal finance—also referred to as lawsuit funding, lawsuit loans, pre-settlement funding, tort advances, plaintiff advances, litigation finance, litigation financing, litigation funding or dispute finance—has inspired its share of controversy over the years. Much of this controversy stems from confusion over the basic principles and practices that define the industry. Through a decade of advancements made by investors, a growing number of lawsuit-related financial products have become available in the United States and other countries. Currently, the legal finance industry offers three main product lines, with companies tending to specialize in each specific product.

First, there is the lawsuit advance for tort claims, which is perhaps the most well-known and often maligned legal finance product. Sometimes referred to as a lawsuit loan or nonrecourse loan, it is provided in the United States and Canada to individual plaintiffs for living expenses, frequently when the plaintiff's ability to work has been affected by an accident. Lawsuit advances furnish plaintiffs with an immediate cash payment they can use for their personal needs, which is intended to improve their chances for enduring protracted litigation, while furthering their chances for a fairer recovery. The market for lawsuit advances is still relatively small, offering opportunities to mostly smaller investors, but has the capacity to grow substantially as rates decline and market acceptance grows.

Second, an increasing number of providers focus on funding commercial matters, which are business disputes brought by individual or corporate plaintiffs in areas such as contracts, intellectual property, antitrust, and banking, among others. Transactions in this space typically provide direct funding for litigation expenses, bridging the gap between what plaintiffs are able or willing to pay and the expected costs of prosecuting commercial lawsuits to resolution. In some cases, capital may be used to fund the working capital of businesses or personal expenses of the business owners. This is a market that offers the greatest promise for larger investors to participate in a vast sector of the economy, while leveling the playing field for numerous participants who were previously unable to use the legal system to make them whole. A large number of these commercial matters are patent infringement claims against large corporations, usually in the technology sector. The patent enforcement niche is one of the oldest legal finance markets in the United States and worldwide. By some estimates, the volume in this market is valued at over $4 billion per year.

Third, a number of companies provide loans to attorneys and law firms. This market developed because contingency law firms have traditionally been underfinanced. Many small and mid-size contingency firms have very thin balance sheets, with most of their receivables tied up in prospective fees. Firms that rely on contingent fees from winning cases are usually self-financing entities that find it challenging to secure financing from traditional lenders who are unable to properly evaluate their collateral. To fill this gap for law firms, a new product was created to help finance litigation, accelerate the repayment of case costs, and cover overhead expenses. Because funding companies deal with the legal industry every day, they have become proficient at valuing the assets of law firms. As a result, they are able to provide much larger loans than a bank ever could, with substantially less personal collateral required. This market has flourished quickly in just a few years, with nearly $1 billion of investments made to contingency law firms all over the country. Growing pains and overzealous underwriting, however, have contributed to a contraction of this market from the wild expansion of its inceptive years. As law firm lending recovers from this contraction, it is poised to provide significant opportunities for larger investors to participate in a multi-billion dollar market.

The origination of legal finance assets on an institutional basis, along with the application of portfolio investment models to the selection of financing prospects, is a relatively new phenomenon. Despite a slow start, the practice of investing capital in lawsuits has grown over the past decade in the United States and other countries. The slowdown of the global economy, combined with tightening credit markets, declining asset values, escalating legal costs, increased backing by institutional investors, and a growing receptivity in the legal industry to innovative financial products, has driven the expansion of this novel and profitable field. What started as a cottage industry in the nineties has evolved into an alternative asset class with growing institutional participation, including several public companies, and an overall greater availability of financial products for individuals, businesses and law firms.

CHAPTER 2
U.S. LEGAL SECTOR

"The United States is the greatest law factory
the world has ever known."

– Charles Evans Hughes, Sr., Chief Justice
of the U.S. Supreme Court
(1930–1941)

Although non-lawyers have had few meaningful opportunities to participate in the economics of the legal sector until very recently, many are all too familiar with the exorbitant costs that legal matters often entail. Most people have interacted with the legal system in some way. Everyone has seen a courtroom drama. Others have experienced it firsthand. For some it's a brush with the law or a motor vehicle accident; for others a matrimonial problem or business dispute. People rely on the courts every day to deliver justice and recognize their importance to a well-functioning society.

Not everyone realizes, however, the sheer scale of this sector.

The U.S. legal industry is vast. Hundreds of billions of dollars are paid out annually by defendants to settle personal injury and commercial claims. Hundreds of billions more are earned by law firms for legal services. The combined value of all verdicts, settlements, attorneys' fees, and billings for non-lawyer legal services would easily eclipse the GDP of Switzerland. The total value of the U.S. legal sector is thought to exceed $700 billion per year.[1]

Each year, U.S. state courts handle approximately 20 million civil cases.[2] The federal courts handled nearly 300,000 more.[3] Many of these cases are from small claims courts, as well as negligence claims and car accidents. They also include the high-stakes battles that occur between corporate giants every year. Many of the larger lawsuits are filed in federal courts.

Tort Law

In the United States, tort litigation is much more common than in other countries, making up a large portion of civil litigation that occurs in state court systems. Americans file over a million tort claims every year. Tort law is a body of law that is used to apportion responsibility for damages that occur as a result of negligence, accidents, and personal injury. In its purest form, imagine a two-car collision between total strangers at an uncontrolled intersection. The drivers have no advance understanding between them as to how they should drive or an agreement specifying who would pay for the damages. The two sides will have different views on what happened and who is responsible. This type of disagreement is settled by courts.

A person who suffers an injury is entitled to receive damages, usually monetary compensation, from the person held responsible for those injuries. Tort law defines what constitutes a legal injury and whether a person may be held liable for an injury they have caused. In addition to physical injuries, legal injuries may also include emotional, economic, or reputational injuries, as well as violations of privacy, property, or constitutional rights.

Damages that result from torts can include wage losses, medical expenses, fire losses, and property damage, among others. The economic impact of these unintentional injuries amounted to almost $700 billion in 2009.[4] For example, there are more than 5 million car accidents[5] and 4 million workplace injuries each year, including 300,000 construction accidents.[6] More than 8 million people are treated each year for slips, trips, and falls.[7] According to the National Safety Council, nearly 40 million injuries occur to people throughout the United States each year that require a doctor's care—while almost 130,000 die from their injuries.[8]

Liability for these incidents is often disputed, frequently leading to personal injury litigation. Estimates place the number of tort cases brought every year in the United States at around 1.2 million for state courts and approximately 100,000 in federal courts, which frequently handle the largest and most complex tort claims.[9] The United States is a country of highways and drivers, with over 250 million cars on the road as of this writing. Not surprisingly, traffic accident claims account for more than half of all tort cases today. Tort litigation can be broken down into three major areas: automobile accidents, medical malpractice, and premises liability.

State tort trials in 75 largest counties, by case type, 2005

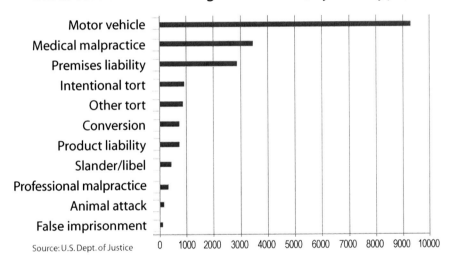

Source: U.S. Dept. of Justice

Despite persistent popular claims that personal injury litigation is excessive in this country, the number of tort claims has actually declined by 25 percent over the past decade.[10] The overall median jury award has also declined by 40 percent since 1992.[11] According to the U.S. Department of Justice, on average, when tort claims proceed to trial, plaintiffs win roughly half the time.[12] In automobile accidents that go to trial, plaintiffs win 64 percent of the time, compared with 23 percent in medical malpractice, and only 19 percent in product liability trials.[13]

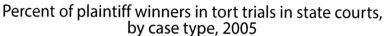

Percent of plaintiff winners in tort trials in state courts, by case type, 2005

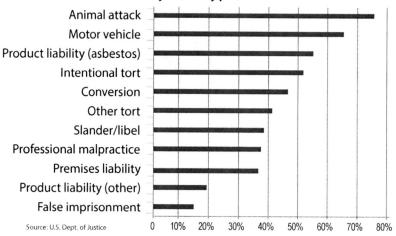

Source: U.S. Dept. of Justice

Tort cases that go to trial have an average length from filing to disposition of approximately 27 months for jury trials and 21 months for bench trials.[14] The median award for all tort cases is $24,000. Automobile related torts have the lowest awards with a median jury award of $15,000. In contrast, medical malpractice and product liability litigation often involve much higher awards. In 2005, the median award won by successful plaintiffs in medical malpractice and product liability cases in state courts was $400,000 and $567,000 respectively.[15]

At the top range, tort verdicts can be quite substantial. In 2011, Exxon Mobil Corporation was hit with a $1.5 billion verdict for contaminating a neighborhood's water supply. The jury awarded $500 million in compensatory damages for emotional distress, loss of property value, and medical monitoring, including steep punitive damages. In another case, a Michigan court awarded $144.6 million to a woman who sued the hospital where she gave birth to a daughter who suffered a brain injury.[16]

Commercial Lawsuits

Many lawsuits occur in a business context. There are many causes for business litigation, but the most common is breach of contract. More than 12 million contract disputes are filed every year.[17] In addition, there are thousands of lawsuits covering such broad areas as intellectual property, antitrust, real estate, banking, securities, insurance, and many others.

The size of the commercial litigation market is difficult to assess. Most lawsuits result in confidential settlements where the exact terms of payment are kept private. Nevertheless, based on the total volume of business litigation, which has increased by 63 percent from 1999 to 2008,[18] the total value of all judgments and settlements is estimated at hundreds of billions of dollars per year.

Compared to tort cases, a higher percentage of plaintiffs prevail at trial in commercial claims. For example, more than 60 percent of plaintiffs win in contract trials.[19] Among the most successful litigants in commercial trials are sellers suing to enforce a contract, winning nearly 75 percent of the time, and business partners who sue to enforce their rights, prevailing approximately 65 percent of the time.[20]

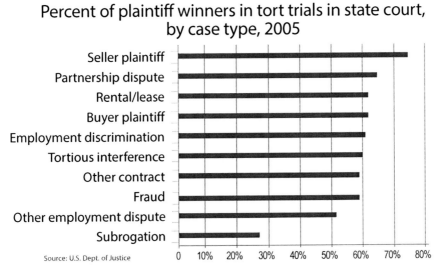

Percent of plaintiff winners in tort trials in state court, by case type, 2005

Source: U.S. Dept. of Justice

Like tort claims, contract cases that go to trial also have an average length from filing to disposition of about 27 months for jury trials and 21 months for bench trials.[21] The median award for all tort cases is $35,000.[22] Contract disputes where the plaintiff is the buyer have the lowest awards with a median jury award of $17,000. In contrast, awards for employment discrimination and tortious interference are significantly higher. In 2005, the median award won by successful plaintiffs in employment discrimination and tortious interference claims in state courts was $175,000 and $169,000, respectively.

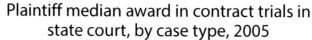

Plaintiff median award in contract trials in state court, by case type, 2005

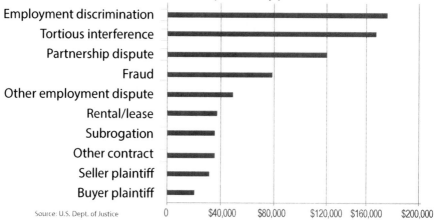

Source: U.S. Dept. of Justice

Statistics from the top 100 verdicts of 2011 reveal much about the current momentum in the system. According to VerdictSearch, the largest verdicts came from intellectual property cases, nearly tripling in value compared with 2010, with 16 verdicts totaling $5.3 billion. One case in the Eastern District of Virginia involves E.I. du Pont de Nemours and Co. against Kolon Industries, Inc. The jury agreed the South Korean company stole numerous trade secrets from DuPont associated with the material Kevlar and awarded DuPont $919.9 million. Another case in the Eastern District of Texas involved a doctor who sued Johnson & Johnson for infringing on his patent for a drug delivery system. He received a $482 million verdict. Fraud verdicts were also significant. In a case brought by the Texas attorney general, court found that

Actavis Group had engaged in inaccurate reporting causing Medicaid to overpay pharmacies for prescription drugs, awarding the state $170.3 million.[23]

Lawyers and Law Firms

As mentioned, attorneys generally earn their fees in one of three ways. Those who specialize in torts for individuals often work on contingency. In such an arrangement, they receive no pay if they do not recover a monetary award for their client. These attorneys often tend to be selective about their clients, and typically receive between 30 percent and 40 percent of the award as their fee. They may also pay for many of the expenses associated with preparing a case for trial—a common practice in tort cases but not business claims.

Some lawyers may work on a flat fee basis, especially for routine engagements. Most attorneys, though, work on retainer and are paid by the hour for their work. All work of any sort is billed to the client, ranging from phone calls to time spent writing letters and conducting research. Fees for attorneys in major U.S. cities often run into the hundreds of dollars per hour.

Where lawyers work in the U.S., 2008

.3% Public interest organizations
.4% Interest groups
.7% Education
5.6% Am. Law Top 50 law firms
8.4% Business
9.1% Rest of National Law Journal 250
15.6% Government
23.6% Other law firms
35.2% Solo Practice

Source: The Legal Finance Journal

Americans have historically maintained a love-hate relationship with the legal profession. On the one hand, lawyers are regarded as advocates, problem solvers, law creators, statesmen, and teachers. They are heralded as champions of freedom and guardians of our individual rights. When a parent is killed in an accident, a child injured by a defective product, a town poisoned by environmental contamination, or an individual wrongfully accused of a crime, lawyers are perceived as indispensable advocates of our public interest and buffers against corporate greed and callousness. On the other hand, lawyers are unceremoniously loathed and condemned. They are the proverbial butt of jokes and targets of fervent and frequent vitriol. Some denounce lawyers for exercising their power for personal gain, often depicting them as too greedy or manipulative, while also criticizing them for gaming the system. Others accuse lawyers of being problem creators rather than problem solvers. Many are displeased with the expense and the perceived waste inherent in our legal system. Still others chastise the legal profession for its elitist and parochial disposition.

The reasons for this dichotomy are multifaceted. Because the United States is founded on principles of law and due process, lawyers wield disproportionate power due to their skill at navigating those laws. The legal profession is broadly represented in government, in business, and in academia. Thirty-three of the fifty-five delegates to the Constitutional Convention were lawyers.[24] There are currently 202 attorneys in Congress.[25] Twenty-five of forty-four U.S. presidents have been lawyers.[26] Many corporate CEOs and top-level executives are also attorneys. Furthermore, legal scholars play a prominent role in shaping the discourse about our system of jurisprudence and civil society in general. The profound level of power enjoyed by lawyers draws praise and admiration while at the same time attracting envy and resentment.

Like medicine and banking, the legal profession is considered special, receiving a great deal of scrutiny from the public as a result. Our popular culture also depends on the legal profession for entertainment value. We have celebrity lawyers, courtroom dramas, and many real-life legal battles that have roused emotions of our citizens throughout the years. The publicity surrounding the legal profession often exposes lawyers for what they are: guardians of our individual liberties, though imperfect and fallible human beings.

Many are incensed by perceptions of lawyers' aloof demeanor. The legal profession is notoriously insular and conservative by nature. Attorneys are cerebral, detached and often narrowly focused in their particular field. They use their own professional jargon—legalese—which may at times seem inaccessible to laypersons. They have their own clubs, trade organizations and lobbying groups. The legal profession is also self-regulating: state bar associations rather than government bodies enforce the canons of ethics and professional responsibility. Each state has its own bar organization, and regulation is conducted on a state-by-state basis. About half of states have an "integrated bar" system, in which an attorney admitted to practice law in that state must become a member of the state bar association. The bar associations in these states have substantial power in terms of admission to practice law, education, and discipline. Lawyers' decisions, even in their personal lives, are made against the backdrop of their regulatory responsibilities.

Lawyers tend to resist change. Their professional lives and practices are replete with formalism, decorum, and anachronistic traditions. Innovation and the use of technology to increase productivity are not as pervasive as they are in other industries. In fact, it is still common to see older practitioners without computers on their desks. Their business models are also slow to modernize. For instance, hourly billing, a practice universally despised by all clients, has been employed ubiquitously for nearly six decades. Another example is the profession's lingering aversion to advertising, which was not permitted until 1977, due to the American Bar Association's traditional view that legal advertising was an unprofessional practice.

The emergence of third-party legal finance has come about at a time when the legal industry is undergoing a titanic transformation. The insular and conservative disposition of lawyers has contributed to the stresses that are now affecting its ranks in the wake of the financial crisis, causing unprecedented changes and producing a painful restructuring in the way legal services are delivered. Lawyers are responding to a number of challenges. The economic downturn produced considerable economic difficulties, including lower earnings, reduced hiring, downsizing, and significant internal reorganization. Emerging trends such as self-help through broad access to legal information online and the automation of many legal tasks via companies such as LegalZoom have made an appreciable dent in firms' revenues.

Clients are also demanding far more control over their relationship with law firms, seeking more efficient services, lower fee structures and a shift away from hourly billing models, as well as increased customer service. These trends have emerged against the background of a hyper-competitive marketplace, which has become more transparent and globalized than ever before. Many of large and even mid-sized law firms now have offices around the world. In this context, competition is fierce and clients will not hesitate to replace their counsel if not satisfied with their service.

Technology has enabled rapid know-how transfer across different jurisdictions and many legal systems are experiencing increasing convergence. Emerging markets like India have made inroads into legal outsourcing and corporate legal departments are increasingly being supported from places like Mumbai.

Jurisdiction shopping has also increased in scale as sophisticated litigants seek to bring and defend lawsuits in venues most advantageous to them. One example is the recent securities and fraud lawsuit against Russia's UralSib Financial Corporation, which due to Russia's weak securities and investor protection laws was brought in New York. Another example is the long battle between Chevron and natives of the Ecuadorian rainforest over pollution

—a case that was moved from New York to Ecuador—resulting in an $18 billion judgment against Chevron.

Breakdown of U.S. legal industry revenue, 2012

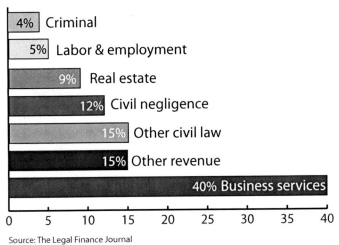

Source: The Legal Finance Journal

Despite these challenges, there is great financial momentum in the system. There are currently tens of thousands of plaintiffs' lawyers who advertise for clients, find cases, and marshal their rights in court. Every year, approximately 180,000 law offices generate nearly $250 billion in revenue.[27]

Top Ten Global Law Firms by Revenue, 2012

Firm	Location	Gross Revenue (in thousands)
Baker & McKenzie	U.S.	$2,313,000
DLA Piper	U.S.	$2,247,000
Skadden, Arps, Slate, Meagher & Flom	U.S.	$2,165,000
Latham & Watkins	U.S.	$2,152,000
Clifford Chance	U.K.	$2,090,500
Linklaters	U.K.	$1,936,000
Allen & Overy	U.K.	$1,898,000
Freshfields Bruckhaus Deringer	U.K.	$1,827,500
Kirkland & Ellis	U.S.	$1,750,000
Hogan Lovells	U.S.	$1,665,000

Source: The American Lawyer

Arbitration

A private legal system where parties resolve their disputes exists in addition to the government-administered legal system. Arbitration is a parallel market of substantial size, although no one truly knows the exact numbers associated with this private dispute resolution mechanism. Like courtroom litigation, arbitration is a process in which the plaintiff and defendant present their case to a third party, usually an arbitrator or panel of arbitrators.[28] As trier of fact and law, the third party will consider all the evidence and then make a binding decision for the parties. Arbitration is generally not as formal as court proceedings and has a much narrower scope of discovery.

Arbitration has emerged as a viable alternative to litigation in the past two decades for a number of reasons. First, unlike the publicity that accompanies lawsuits in courts, arbitration is private. This may be an attractive feature to litigants that require confidentiality. Second, arbitration is generally much faster and cheaper than court adjudication. Informal rules and the binding, non-appealable nature of arbitration decisions have the effect of reducing time to disposition by streamlining the dispute resolution process. Finally, parties to arbitration can generally select their own arbitrators, which may be particularly valuable in cases where the subject matter is highly technical or complex.

In the United States, arbitration is primarily used in commercial, consumer, and labor-management disputes. It has become the standard in securities disputes among brokers, as well as between financial firms and their customers. It is also used extensively for labor disputes, primarily in the context of collective bargaining agreements for professional sports and labor unions. Courts may resort to arbitration as well, particularly in family law cases, where judges may require arbitration for child custody hearings.

Arbitration has become increasingly common for resolving international business disputes, especially for parties that prefer not to use their own courts because they are expensive, function poorly, or may be susceptible to graft. International arbitration provides the parties with a neutral forum, leveling the playing field for litigants. Many international contracts specify that arbitration should be used to resolve any disputes that arise from that agreement. Frequently, the contract also names a particular dispute resolution body. This kind of arbitration usually takes place at the New York-based International Centre for Dispute Resolution (ICDR), the London Court of International Arbitration (LCIA), the Paris-based International Chamber of Commerce (ICC), the Arbitration Institute of the Stockholm Chamber of Commerce (SCC), the Hong Kong International Arbitration Centre (HKIAC), and other similar organizations around the world. Decisions issued by these bodies are binding on the litigants and enforceable in their home countries if they are signatories to the New York Convention, which in 1958 harmonized the recognition of foreign arbitral awards among most nations.[29]

The types of cases brought before these tribunals vary, but generally include complex commercial matters, often involving multiple jurisdictions. These matters are often large and the amounts in dispute often run into hundreds of millions or even billions of dollars. According to the LCIA, 25 percent of the claims filed in 2008 included damage claims of more than $5 million, while the ICC reported a sharp rise in the number of high-value claims in the same year, with 31 filings for damages of more than $100 million and four involving amounts in excess of $1 billion.[30] Arbitrated cases also tend to settle, although not with the same frequency as claims adjudicated in court. The majority of international arbitration claims receive a decision from the arbitration panel, primarily because the consequences of adverse decisions are more manageable in the context of arbitration compared to a court adjudicated dispute.

There has been a dramatic rise in international arbitration during the past 20 years. For instance, the LCIA reported a 55 percent increase in new claims between 2007 and 2008, and double digit gains in the following years. Similar trends have also been observed in other major arbitration forums around the world.[31]

Do Most Cases Settle?

> "A lawsuit is a machine which you go into as a pig and come out as a sausage."
>
> *– Ambrose Gwinnett Bierce (1842-1913)*
> *American journalist, The Devil's Dictionary*

The emerging legal finance industry attempts to forecast the outcome of cases in a landscape where the large majority of lawsuits are resolved out of court or through arbitration. A study conducted by the U.S. Department of Justice concluded, among other things, that only 2 percent of the 762,000 cases disposed of—whether by settlement or trial—are decided by juries.[32] The remaining cases are either dismissed, fail to proceed, or privately resolved among the parties through settlement.

This does not mean that every plaintiff wins their lawsuit, much less receives the full amount of their claim. In fact, the majority of cases are settled for just a fraction of the plaintiff's initial demand. Many factors can contribute to strengthening or weakening a lawsuit. Financial considerations will play a central role in any decision. For many potential claims, the costs of bringing a lawsuit will exceed the expected recovery, either because the chances of winning are low, or because the plaintiff's damages are too small. Cases may be dismissed along the way or never properly litigated. The circumstances of the case or parties may change as the case develops.

The cases that do proceed will be subject to numerous events that can change the fortunes of either party. The incentive to settle, therefore, is uncertainty. When disputants go to trial, control passes from the parties to the hands of the judge and jury. A jury may have difficulty understanding the complexities of the case, the award may be vastly different from the amount anticipated, and litigation can consume considerable time and resources. With clogged judicial dockets and soaring legal expenses, it is unsurprising that most civil cases never reach a jury.

In its most simplified form, a trial has two possible outcomes: a "win" or a "loss." Discovery, pre-trial motions, and summary judgment rulings generally help clarify the merits and value of a claim prior to trial and encourage settlement by the parties. The probability of winning may be assessed on the basis of an evaluation of the merits of the case, prior experience with the type of case, and other factors.

During this process, litigants constantly adjust strategies in response to new information that develops during the course of the lawsuit. They may consider several factors when faced with the choice of proposing or accepting a settlement offer versus the prospect of proceeding with litigation. Important among such factors are the chances of success at trial, the likely duration of the trial, the expected size of an award, the likelihood of an appeal, and expected litigation costs. In each case, litigants have their own subjective assessments about the likelihood of success and the likely duration of the litigation process.

By some estimates, nearly 40 percent of all tort claims and a similar percentage of commercial cases in the United States are never filed in court. Millions of cases are not counted by the legal system because they are never formally commenced. The aggrieved party may hire a lawyer to champion their cause, but the actual lawsuit never proceeds because it is either abandoned or settled out of court. In a motor vehicle claim, for example, it is common practice for attorneys to first gather evidence and then send a demand package to the insurance adjustor. In many cases where the merits are well-established, defendants pay without litigation.

Conclusion

By any measurable rubric, the U.S. legal sector is massive. Within its courtrooms each year are tens of millions of cases—a good proportion of the civil docket comprised of torts and commercial lawsuits—and hundreds of billions of dollars change hands. Attorneys occupy a dichotomized position within the sector, both celebrated and hated for their important role in the legal system. Arbitration, settlement, and other out-of-court forms of resolution represent a substantial proportion of tort and commercial claims—as much as 40 percent by some estimates—that are never formally initiated, and thus unfold in addition to courtroom statistics. A market of this staggering size and magnitude cannot help but offer a compelling investment proposition.

CHAPTER 3

LEGAL FINANCE PRODUCTS

Lawsuit Advances for Tort Plaintiffs

After their debilitating car accident, Tim and Caroline need an interim funding solution to replace lost income and meet their pressing financial obligations. How will they afford basic necessities like food, rent, mortgage, car payments, and medical bills? Finding a personal or payday loan will be difficult for Tim, as banks do not provide loans to the unemployed or to those with marginal credit and no collateral. Friends and family may help with some expenses in the short term, but for most plaintiffs this option is not available.

If Tim asks his lawyer for a loan, he will discover that ethics rules prohibit attorneys from providing money to their clients because such transactions may lead to conflicts of interest. According to the ABA Rules of Professional Conduct, lawyers are prohibited from lending money to clients with the exception of advancing court costs and expenses of litigation.[1] Many states have adopted similar standards.

This couple's troubles are far from unique. Every year, millions of Americans are injured through the negligence of others. With their ability to work hindered, many find themselves unable to support their families. In cases of personal injury, victims may also need to pay for medical bills not covered by insurance. Even when lawsuits are eventually filed against the responsible parties, proceedings can drag on for years. Without a temporary lifeline, many victims risk financial ruin in their fight for justice.

Defendants who are repeat players in personal injury litigation are keenly aware of the problems plaintiffs face. Those defendants have an incentive to prolong litigation, commonly using delay tactics like excessive motion and discovery requests. In fact, the higher the stakes, the more incentive a defendant has to wage a costly war of attrition that most plaintiffs are ill-prepared to bear. Predictably, financial pressure often leads to suboptimal outcomes for plaintiffs because it creates strong incentives to settle for far less than their cases are worth.

Some plaintiffs rely on personal loans, credit cards, or savings to cover living expenses while pursuing their lawsuits. Traditional types of financing like these may be available in limited circumstances, but they also create problems of their own. For example, loans and credit cards require employment verifications and credit checks. They also involve an absolute repayment requirement—usually a monthly payment commencing immediately, regardless of the recipient's ability to repay them.

Upon exhausting all other options, the only way Tim is likely to obtain additional funds is through a cash advance from a legal finance provider against the future proceeds of his lawsuit. This lawsuit-linked financial product allows plaintiffs like Tim to meet their daily expenses before the resolution of their claims. Sometimes called "pre-settlement funding," "lawsuit loans," "tort advances," or "lawsuit advances," cash advances for tort claims are not actually loans—they are upfront cash payments to the plaintiff in return for a promise by the plaintiff to pay the investor a portion of any future proceeds from that claim.

Tort advances can relieve the financial pressure for plaintiffs who have no other options for financing everyday bills. The funds can be used to pay for housing, groceries, and family emergencies, among other things. Lawsuit advances can help to sustain plaintiffs throughout protracted legal battles, improving their prospects for receiving larger, fairer compensation.

An interesting development in the past two years has been the increased financing of medical procedures by legal finance companies. Many victims of personal injury are unable to receive necessary medical procedures because they have no insurance or defendants' insurance refuses to pay until liability has been established. Due to the high cost and inefficiency of our medical system, the financing of medical procedures will continue to gain momentum.

Unlike loans, lawsuit advances do not require applicants to have jobs, collateral, or good credit. In fact, funding companies rarely evaluate people's credit worthiness. Instead, they focus almost exclusively on the quality of the underlying claims, which have no inherent value unless and until the plaintiff recovers compensation. Lawsuit advances are also not factoring transactions. Unlike factoring, where a legal right already exists, lawsuit advances allow plaintiffs to receive money long before defendants are legally compelled to make any payment. Lawsuit advances do not require any personal guarantees and will not appear on the clients' credit report. They do not increase the recipients' net debt obligations or monthly payments.

To be eligible for this type of funding, plaintiffs must have:

1. a viable legal claim,
2. against solvent defendants,
3. as a result of a verifiable personal injury (or other personal tort),
4. in a jurisdiction that does not prohibit lawsuit advances, and
5. be represented by a qualified and properly licensed attorney on a contingency basis.

The most important feature of lawsuit advances is their non-recourse nature. Recipients have no obligation to repay if their claims never proceed or are lost or dismissed. The amount of a plaintiff's recovery is also a ceiling on any payments that must be made to the funding company. The attorney will repay the advance after receiving funds from the defendant or insurance company, either as a result of a negotiated settlement or court verdict. Unlike loans, there are no interim payments.

Eligible claims should be free from any serious encumbrances such as prior funding, judgments, or excessive medical liens. Plaintiffs' attorneys must be experienced in the relevant area of the law, have an acceptable record of professional conduct, and should be cooperative with the investment process.

After the investment is made, funders do not participate in managing the underlying litigation. The funding agreements do not confer any right to direct or influence the process in any way. The legal strategy for litigation and the decision to accept a particular outcome is solely within the control of plaintiffs and their attorneys. Funders receive periodic updates regarding the development of cases and typically find out about settlements, verdicts, and losses only after they happen. Furthermore, lawsuit advances do not transfer or assign from plaintiffs to funders any right to sue on their behalf. They merely establish an agreement to transfer portions of any future proceeds received from the lawsuits.

Upon resolution of a case, any moneys recovered from settlement or adjudication are received directly by the attorney and deposited into the firm's escrow account, which holds the settlement funds before any distributions are made to the client.[2] This mitigates counterparty risk by requiring that investors be paid first.

The convenience of lawsuit advances comes at a steep price tag. Most funding companies charge between 40 and 80 percent per year in fees that operate like compound interest—causing the plaintiff's obligation to increase quickly. Plaintiffs whose cases remain unresolved for a greater period of time will generally see a larger percentage of their recovery go toward paying the funding company.

Even though rates have come down substantially since the industry's Wild West days, factors such as high origination and processing costs, as well as the risks associated with losses, reductions, and staggered cash flow—given that most cases are resolved in a year or more with no interim payments from clients—continually limit the industry's ability to reduce rates. Despite efforts by legal finance companies to bring down the costs of funding over the years, their funding sources continue to demand high premiums for credit facilities, in part due to the lingering stigma and uncertainty associated with lawsuit advances. Nevertheless, acceptance of this product will only increase among plaintiffs as rates continue their decline. As the legal framework evolves in the direction of greater acceptance and technology yields advances in productivity and efficiency, the cost of lawsuit advances will diminish inevitably as well.

The market for tort advances is still relatively small compared to the total amount of tort litigation in the United States and the scale of other financial products. The *New York Times* estimates that about $100 million in advances are made every year,[3] while other estimates run as high as $300 million. Even using the highest figures, advances account for less than 0.1 percent of total tort verdicts and settlements in the United States every year. By contrast, the annual market for car loans is about $30 billion,[4] and JP Morgan Chase made approximately $47 billion in mortgage loans in the third quarter of 2012 alone.[5]

Several factors contribute to this market's low volume. One of the most notable among them is that the high fees related to lawsuit advances discourage many people from seeking this type of funding—often to their detriment. If fees were lower, many more plaintiffs would use this product to bridge the financial gap until they recover compensation from defendants.

The small size of each funding transaction also contributes to the industry's modest funding volume. Lawsuit investors will usually advance no more than 15 percent of the estimated net value of a claim, after adjusting for attorneys' fees and liens. Since the value of a personal injury claim averages under $30,000, the size of the average investment is also relatively small—under $5,000. Personal injury lawsuits are also not as ubiquitous as home or car ownership. Even if parties file more than a million lawsuits every year, plaintiffs in personal injury lawsuits represent a very small percentage of the general population at any given time. Moreover, only about a third of them have pressing financial difficulties that require third-party funding. While this market refreshes itself every year, few people have more than one or two personal injury claims in their lifetime. Repeat business seldom occurs.

The small size of the market is also partly a result of attorney reticence. Unlike other financial products—or most products in general—legal finance deals cannot be consummated without the explicit cooperation of attorneys. Not only do they provide critical background information about claims to underwriters, they also have to approve the deal and agree to perform the role of an escrow agent. Unfortunately, many attorneys simply refuse to cooperate with their clients' requests for advances because they view them as an encumbrance rather than a resource. Others are concerned about taking on additional responsibilities, while many are concerned about the high fees associated with legal finance products. As a result, attorneys preclude many deals that could otherwise obtain funding.

The tort advance market has become very competitive in the last few years, and the number of cases available for investment has not kept pace with available capital. Approximately 200 companies currently provide lawsuit cash advances, with most advertising their services online. The majority of these companies are brokers who originate cases for the approximately 40 companies across the country which serve as primary funders. Of these, about half are members of the American Legal Finance Association (ALFA), a trade association that oversees funding activities in legal finance, primarily in the tort space (although some member companies also fund commercial cases to a lesser extent).

The leaders in this space include Oasis, LawCash, Peachtree Pre-Settlement Funding, PS Finance, and Golden Pear Funding. The ALFA website provides a good resource for identifying the most active companies in this field.[6]

Nine funding companies established ALFA in 2004 to help promote and maintain appropriate ethical standards and fair business practices within the legal finance industry. The organization also strives to increase awareness of the industry and to establish a legal and regulatory framework in individual states that meet the needs of all parties involved in legal finance transactions.

Despite growing popularity, tort advances have not yet reached the same level of ubiquity as more mainstream financial products. Even as they become more pervasive, their relatively modest funding size will prevent them from becoming a sizeable market like mortgages and automotive finance. For this reason, they do not currently offer significant investment opportunities for large investors, as the ability to deploy significant capital in this space remains a considerable challenge. For smaller investors, though, tort advances present a compelling risk-return proposition in a generally uncorrelated market.

Legal Finance for Business Disputes

In our second example, Susan's company was damaged by a supplier's defective product. Her company could file a lawsuit against the supplier—a case they are almost certain to win—but the firm's financial woes prevent them from suing unless they can secure financing. The stakes are high: a victory could revive the moribund manufacturer, giving it the resources to regain its competitiveness and access new markets, while a poorly conceived effort might precipitate the firm's demise.

Susan could try to find an accomplished commercial attorney to take her case on contingency. However, finding a skilled, experienced, and well-resourced attorney on contingency will not be easy. The incentive models in most firms discourage litigation funding.

Commercial litigators tend to shy away from contingency arrangements, preferring to bill their clients by the hour. In a typical firm, the attorney hierarchy is determined by annual billings and revenue per partner, associate, etc. A ledger full of contingency matters shifts resources away from the firm, creating a cost center. With an engrained culture programmed to exact hourly fees from their clients regardless of outcomes, commercial litigators loathe to accrue case risk on their balance sheets. Recent publicity regarding the changing models of legal compensation has done little to encourage law firms to take on greater risk for the cases they handle. While some firms have developed bigger appetites for alternative payment structures—including flat fees, bartering equity for legal services, etc.—most still pay the rent by billing out their time to clients.

While most law firms prefer current pay arrangements to contingent fees, exceptions to this rule abound. Several wealthy and successful contingency firms—primarily self-financed from previous wins—do handle commercial claims. These firms are in short supply and very selective about the cases they accept. They tend to narrowly specialize in certain types of claims like antitrust or class-action litigation. Even if Susan is successful in finding such a firm, however, most business lawyers with contingency practices will only invest their professional time. She would still be responsible for expert witness fees, discovery costs, travel, and hundreds of other expenses.

Furthermore, litigation can consume much of her company's productive time, likely exacerbating the company's precarious situation by shifting attention away from revenue generating activities. Contingency arrangements cannot address this problem. What Susan's firm really needs is a cash injection from an investor to pay for the litigation costs, while also providing a much needed insurance policy against unforeseen financial difficulties that can result from litigation.

In the past few years, this type of dispute funding has become increasingly available. Businesses like Susan's company can now take their cases to investors who may agree to pay for some or all the costs of litigation in return for a stake in the lawsuit's future proceeds. In a typical transaction, third-party funding allows plaintiffs to finance most or all of the legal expenses associated with their lawsuits. It is generally available for funding business disputes such as intellectual property and contract claims, as well as shareholder, insurance, bank, securities, and anti-trust litigation.

Commercial legal finance, often called "litigation funding" or "litigation finance," is in essence venture capital for lawsuits. Unlike tort advances, commercial products are intended to fund litigation costs rather than living expenses, although a large minority of cases also provides some capital to business owners for their personal use. Frequently, the funding facility may also be used for the plaintiff's working capital and can help finance a company's growth. In certain circumstances, a deal may also include the outright purchase of the entire claim, a purchase of an interest in an asset that is the subject of litigation (e.g., patents, accounts receivable, etc.), and the making of loans to law firms to finance a portfolio of cases being marshaled by that firm.

Commercial deals also tend to be much larger than tort advances, ranging from several hundred thousand for smaller claims to tens of millions of dollars for some of the world's highest stakes litigation. Due to the disparate nature of commercial lawsuits, however, funding structures in this space possess a high degree of variation. Numerous considerations like the size of the claim, tax matters, ethical and jurisdictional issues, as well as counterparty risks will often drive the investment structure.

There is no streamlined application process. Commercial funders are very selective (and secretive), as only about 5 percent of all matters submitted for underwriting receive funding. Nevertheless, investors generally seek similar characteristics from their investment opportunities. To qualify for funding the investment prospect must have the following:

(1) a viable legal claim with clear liability,

(2) against well-capitalized defendants,

(3) as a result of clear and quantifiable damages,[7]

(4) in a jurisdiction that does not prohibit legal finance,

(5) with representation by an accomplished legal team on a contingency or current pay basis.

Legal finance offers a compelling value proposition for any company, large or small. Capital provided by lawsuit investors is off–balance sheet and non-recourse, allowing businesses to hedge litigation risks using custom-tailored financing solutions not available through conventional commercial lenders. These financial products may also be used to supplement working capital and to remove liabilities from a company's balance sheet. A start-up may need to finance the costs of bringing a lawsuit, while also unlocking additional value from the claim to help fund its growth. For a larger entity, legal finance can help mitigate the risks of lawsuit cost overruns by transferring some of that risk to a repeat player. In fact, many recent legal finance deals have included a number of Fortune 1000 companies, FT Global 500 firms, as well as several universities.

In addition to a lawsuit war chest, funders also bring litigation experience to the mix, offering invaluable insight and litigation management expertise to their clients. As repeat players, funding companies have a unique perspective of the legal system and are better equipped to navigate the various stages of litigation. Free from emotional entanglements that may affect plaintiffs' decision-making process, funders can provide critical objectivity to the litigation strategy. They understand what is necessary to bring a successful action and are expert at setting litigation budgets, controlling expenses, and evaluating procedural milestones. They can also contribute important resources like legal experts, risk and financial analysts, collection specialists, and international expertise. By leveraging the unique capabilities that funding companies bring to the dispute resolution process, plaintiffs can increase their prospects for a favorable outcome.

Like tort advances, investments are made in one or several tranches (portions). If the deal requires several tranches to fund follow-on investments as the case develops, investors will retain the right to terminate the financing arrangement if new developments negatively impact their chances for a recovery.

Once lawsuit investors become involved, their role within the litigation process varies. Depending on their investment strategy, funders can exercise different degrees of control, ranging from completely passive to active participation in formulating strategy and making vital decisions. After the investment is made, funders will typically communicate with plaintiffs and their legal team on a regular basis to monitor the development of the claim. Despite these varying levels of involvement, however, investors rarely instruct the legal team directly or participate in the day-to-day management of cases.

If the structure of the deal involves paying for litigation expenses and, especially in situations where the plaintiff retains counsel on a current pay basis, most investors will want to ensure that their investment will be sufficient to cover all of the projected expenses.[8] After all, if the case runs out of money, the funder's investment in that claim will be held hostage until they or someone else agrees to provide further funding. To protect themselves against this scenario, investors will usually take part in the formulation of a litigation budget, which they will closely oversee to mitigate any cost overruns. They may even cap lawyers' fees to further align the litigation budget and strategy.

At the same time, funders take steps to confirm that plaintiffs spend their investment proceeds on actual litigation expenses. If a plaintiff receives funding to finance expert witness costs but instead spends the money on working capital for his business, the funder will almost certainly have a very serious problem.[9] For this reason, funders will frequently appoint an escrow agent—usually another attorney or law firm—to disburse the investment funds directly to service providers in accordance with the terms of the agreement.

Ultimately, the claimants' cooperation is the mainstay of the litigation process. Funding companies, therefore, require claimants to cooperate with their counsel and devote sufficient time to conclude the lawsuit. To further align plaintiffs' interests, funders will leave them with substantial portions of their lawsuits, providing an economic incentive that will ensure future cooperation. Their obligation to cooperate will also be detailed in the investment agreement. Plaintiffs are expected to consult with their legal team about all matters related to their claim. They must provide all necessary documentation supporting their cases and make themselves available for the preparation of written statements, subscribing to them under oath if necessary. They must also appear at any hearings and provide testimony. If they fail to cooperate, they will usually become personally liable to their funders for any losses.

Technically, only plaintiffs have the capacity to decide whether to settle their claims, although some companies attempt to structure various levers in their agreements to give themselves direct or constructive veto powers over such decisions.[10] In practice, however, any settlement offer must be a collaborative decision among the client, the law firm, and the investor.

Like other lawsuit-linked products, legal finance for business disputes is expensive. Many investors charge a threefold or fourfold return, while some have even higher expectations for their capital, perhaps as a result of riskier investment strategies. Some deals may be structured as a percentage of the recovery, similar to attorney contingent fees. Others use a blended approach, combining a fixed return with a percentage of the recovery. Regardless of the structure, it is not unusual to see target annualized returns exceeding 100 percent per annum.

Despite increasing interest in this field and the recent entrance of several hedge funds, the commercial litigation funding market is still in its infancy. As in the tort cash advance space, legal uncertainties have long prevented any meaningful experimentation with this asset class. While it has been a recognized investment type in Australia and the United Kingdom for more than a decade, the much-larger U.S. market is only now starting to see significant capital flow into this space.

In the late nineties, companies specializing in lawsuit advances for tort cases made the first commercial investments. Companies like LawMax, Cambridge, and Plaintiff Support Services each funded dozens of commercial claims, applying essentially the same formula for business disputes as tort cases, focusing on smaller matters with contingency arrangements in place. Most of the capital provided was used to pay for working capital or personal expenses. The typical investment at that time was under $100,000, as most companies lacked the capital base or underwriting methodologies for larger investments.

Today, about a dozen companies currently specialize in commercial litigation around the world, many of them from the United Kingdom. The largest of these firms—Juridica, Burford, and Parabellum Capital—specialize in funding large claims, requiring investments of $5 million or more. Other companies focus on smaller cases, including Bentham Capital,[11] Juris Funding, Black-Robe, Fulbrook Management,[12] Harbour Litigation Funding, Calunius Capital, and our company, LexStone Capital. In addition, companies such as Lighthouse Financial, U.S. Claims, and Incline Energy fund cases requiring $250,000 or less.[13]

The commercial funding field grows rapidly as new entrants appear regularly. One of the primary reasons lawsuit assets attract investors is because they are perceived to be uncorrelated with debt, equity, currency, or commodity markets. This asset class also offers an attractive investment proposition for those who need to deploy substantial capital. Because each investment is generally larger than $250,000, this market offers scalability opportunities for larger investors.

Legal Finance for Intellectual Property

In one of our examples, young inventor Jonathan spent several years developing a communication standard for electronic devices only to see a large tech company enter the market with the very same idea he patented. Jonathan's lawyer informed him that he has a compelling patent infringement claim, but that it will cost him $3 million or more to bring it. Patent cases, however, are almost never accepted by law firms on contingency. How can Jon protect his invention if he lacks the money to fund the lawsuit?

Luckily for Jonathan, intellectual property enforcement is the most developed segment of legal finance and has been around for more than thirty years. Capital is widely available for valuable patents where the technology is being violated by affluent companies.

Intellectual property investing is generally similar to investing in commercial cases, although certain nuances related to this area make it a special category. Unlike other forms of legal finance, patent transfer and enforcement by third parties—which accounts for the overwhelming majority of deals—is allowed by U.S. federal law.[14] For this reason, an active market has developed, with more than $4 billion in annual deal volume.[15] Many transactions in this field involve the outright purchase of patents from the owner rather than an agreement to divide the proceeds upon settlement.

Firms in this space—such as Altitude, Acacia, Eton Park, General Patent, Rembrandt, and Invesco—focus on enforcing intellectual property rights by sending notice letters to companies suspected of infringing those rights. In many cases, funders will license their intellectual property rights to the user without litigation. Lawsuits are generally filed only as a last resort. Many will remember the 2006 case where a Virginia firm called NTP threatened to shut down RIM's BlackBerry service until it agreed to pay more than $600 million to settle the lawsuit. In addition to patents, other intellectual property rights may include monetization of trademarks, brands, trade secrets, royalty streams, copyrights and other intangible assets.

Legal Finance for Contingency Law Firms

The problems found in Anne and David's law firm representing low income mothers are typical of the difficulties many attorneys face. Law firms that specialize in tort claims and work on contingency often find that they have taken on large, potentially lucrative cases, but lack the resources to properly litigate them for a number of reasons. Perhaps a case is more expensive to develop than anticipated. Maybe the firm's settlements are not resolving to keep pace with expenses. Different firms may have different reasons for needing additional financing.

Capital constraints can devastate lawsuits, leading to premature settlements or other undesired results for plaintiffs. Specialized financing, therefore, is necessary in abundance to bring important cases to conclusion. Outside of the legal field, companies usually have numerous options to finance their businesses, from offering securities—like stocks and bonds—to borrowing funds from banks and other institutional lenders. Law firms, however, do not have the same range of options.

For example, in the United States, current ethical rules prohibit non-attorneys from taking ownership interests in law firms, significantly restricting the use of equity securities as a funding option. This prohibition stems primarily from ubiquitous U.S. state laws that outlaw fee-splitting with non-lawyers. These laws are intended to prevent conflicts of interest that may arise when unrelated third parties are in a position to influence litigation as a result of their financial stake in the outcome of the claim. Perennial proposals to lift this restriction have only begun to gain momentum among some members of the ABA.

On rare occasions, debt securities are also used to finance law firms. But they are in generally only available to the largest firms—those with impressive balance sheets and ability to afford the high underwriting fees.

Even large firms typically rely on bank loans and partners' contributions. This reluctance to raise capital from outside investors is often the product of a conservative culture that is prevalent across many law firms. Many may also be uncomfortable about publicity surrounding their financing habits, concerned of the potential stigma it could create among their clients, peers, defendants, and the judiciary.

Although lawyers are prohibited from fee splitting, and issuing securities remains difficult, they are nevertheless permitted to borrow money. Bank financing has historically been the wellspring of the legal sector, particularly for firms generating most of their revenue from current-pay billing arrangements like hourly billing and flat fees. However, firms that rely on contingent fees from winning cases are generally self-financing entities that find it difficult to secure sufficient financing from banks that are unable to understand and evaluate their collateral.

Many small and even mid-size contingency firms have very thin balance sheets, with most of their receivables tied up in prospective fees. Traditional lenders, however, specialize in underwriting balance sheet assets—tangible things that can be secured, foreclosed and sold. They lack the core expertise to determine the value of legal matters, especially contingent ones.

Banks are also unsure of how to handle this type of collateral. They require liquid assets: stocks, bonds, a house, a car, furniture, or some other asset that they can sell in the market. But in the event of default by a law firm, they cannot foreclose on the attorneys' fees and take over the cases. For this reason, they do not accept cases or attorneys' fees as collateral and demand personal guarantees from the firms' partners for any loans they provide.

As a result, most contingency firms are self-financing, having only small bank lines of credit or no bank credit at all. They generally rely on either fee sharing with other law firms, partner's contributions, or credit card debt. Law firms, therefore, are historically underserved by capital markets and as a result pay comparably higher rates to finance their operations than businesses in other industries.

In many cases, the argument for a law firm to take a case on contingency is quite compelling, often due to the enormous financial gain the law firm would realize from a favorable outcome. However, the contingency arrangement often compounds the financial limitations of plaintiffs—who have less-than-perfect access to information about the general capabilities of law firms—with the practical constraints of under-resourced law firms.

For undercapitalized law firms facing a complex and expensive lawsuit, the traditional but rarely publicized solution has been to partner with a rich law firm that will finance the expenses associated with the claim in return for a sizable participation in the contingent fee. A good example of how this works was portrayed in the movie *Erin Brockovich*. Brockovich's firm, Masry & Vititoe, faced the daunting task of litigating with the behemoth Pacific Gas and Electric (PG&E), which could "paper" them to death. Masry knew that a small law firm could not possibly handle the logistical and financial demands of litigating against such a formidable opponent. PG&E had the capacity to outlast them in a war of attrition, which defines most complex litigation today.

So to help pursue the claim on behalf of Hinkley's residents, Masry brought in the fictional character of Kurt Potter, who would supply a war chest for their lawsuit. In real life, Masry & Vititoe partnered with at least two prominent plaintiff's firms, Engstrom, Lipscomb & Lack, and Girardi & Keese, firms that financed more than $12 million of expenses related to the PG&E litigation in return for portion of the legal fee that resulted from that case.[16]

While this type of arrangement offers some benefits to the smaller firm, like subject matter expertise, the use of additional staff, and the absence of credit underwriting by the sponsoring firm (particularly helpful if the smaller firm has bad credit), it remains a very expensive way to finance litigation. In fact, the effective interest rate for these types of deals can be as much as 150 percent per year when you consider the size of the fee split most attorneys are paying these banker law firms.[17]

Credit cards are also frequently used to finance contingent-fee practices, particularly when the attorney is just starting out. In fact, law firms often have $100,000 or more in credit card debt. This type of financing, however, has become less available after the financial crisis, and requires the attorney to keep applying for new cards to increase their credit limit. In addition, credit card companies require good credit and personal guarantees from the business owners.[18]

By far the most common way to finance contingency practices is with partners' cash. This is often done without a conscious decision by the partners to lend their firm money, and is usually done interest-free. As expenses come up, they are paid out of the firm's after-tax money, reducing the profits for the entire practice. This is particularly problematic for case expenses, which are traditionally paid by contingency firms on behalf of their clients in tort claims. For attorneys who have been practicing for a while, the amount of their cash tied up in case expenses could be substantial—a cycle that continues for the life of the firm.[19] As a result, the opportunity cost of not using that money to build personal net worth can be significant.

In this context, the contingency law firm could benefit from some type of third-party investment product to help pay for the expenses of costly legal battles and finance the firm through the lean times. To fill this liquidity gap for law firms, a new legal finance product was created to help finance litigation. Attorneys now have access to a number of lenders that provide this type funding. Several of them are affiliated with companies that cut their teeth in the tort advance market for personal injury victims.

For the investor, however, caveat emptor still applies. Many of the products targeting subprime attorneys and law firms are some of the riskiest investments in legal finance and require a great deal of sophistication and perseverance to manage. These are hands on investments, with high probabilities of default and significant after-the-fact collections, litigation and other servicing expenses. They are not for legal finance novices. The risk associated with each investment is discussed separately according to the type of law firm funding product.

Law firm funding deals can have many different features and are typically bespoke products that meet the specific needs of the law firm. They can be categorized into four different products, all of which have similar features. These products include: (1) contingent advances, (2) lines of credit, (3) case expense loans, and (4) post-settlement funding or fee acceleration.

Contingent advances are made by specialty funding companies to law firms against their fees in one or several cases that have not yet settled. In a typical transaction, the investor will evaluate the firm's cases and arrive at a maximum investment that can be made on the basis of those claims.

If the cases have good prospects for success, the funding company will generally offer approximately 15 to 25 percent of the attorneys' fees relating to those matters. In some instances, where the prospects are particularly compelling and the timing to disposition short, the funding company may increase the advance ratio, but generally will not go above 50 percent.

These types of deals can be structured in different ways. These are typically non-recourse advances, without any personal guarantees or other encumbrances on the firm's other assets. Some are structured as purchases of future fees at a discount. Some deals require the attorney to replace compromised cases with new cases that have similar prospects for recovery, primarily in situations when the attorney is fired or ceases representation.

Regardless of the structure, this type of funding is extremely expensive. The average rates for contingent deals range from 40 to 150 percent per annum. Despite the cost, this type of funding can be an important financing tool for the contingency attorney with limited borrowing power. For those that have few cases, encumbered assets, bad credit or other complicating factors, contingent deals can unlock liquidity that otherwise would remain unproductive for years, generally with very little credit underwriting or due diligence.

On the underwriting side, contingency deals are easy for attorneys to qualify for because of limited disclosure requirements. The partners' credit reports are often overlooked by the investors and the firms' financials generally disregarded. In addition, lawsuit investors often do not report these deals through the filing of a lien, which may be attractive to a law firm that does not want its assets publicly encumbered.

Contingent deals allow law firms to expand by hiring staff or taking on new cases. They can help with emergencies or other pressing personal obligations. They can also finance unexpected expenses associated with lucrative cases, where the prospective fees can more than make up for the high cost of funding. Whatever the reason, contingency deals are often fast and easy, with few questions asked.

Many companies have dabbled in this space, including some of the better known tort advance providers, including Oasis, LawCash, and Cambridge. However, from the investors' perspective, these types of deals are probably the riskiest transactions in the legal finance industry and, as a result of frequent defaults, are less available today than they were only a few years ago.

The probability of client default in this space is significantly higher than any other legal finance investment. Historical defaults exceed 40 percent, and some companies have seen as many as 75 percent of their attorney contingency deals default—mostly as a result of attorney misrepresentation, circumvention, malfeasance and even outright fraud.

The reasons for these results are not difficult to understand. The rates for this product are high because the deals are non-recourse to the attorney's personal or other business assets. If all or many of the cases in the basket fail, the funding company will have to forfeit its investment or accept a significantly reduced payment. But what kind of attorneys would agree to pay 100 percent per year for financing? The answer is usually subprime candidates that have nowhere else to turn, either because they have bad credit, liens, judgments, previous disciplinary suspensions, or some other problem that they are not disclosing. These are typically high risk individuals who are bad at managing money and have already defaulted on previous deals with other funders.

Most of such deals have traditionally required little disclosure. Many funding companies did not—and new entrants still do not—pull credit reports in these deals or conduct background research regarding the firm and its principals. Instead, they had focused on underwriting the underlying cases to assess the appropriate size of investment and the prospects of being repaid from those cases. The common wisdom was that if the advance to value ratio was low enough, then the prospects for default were manageable. Counterparty risk, or the risk that attorneys would simply not pay, even after resolving cases successfully, is usually not part of the evaluation.

In reality, however, this type of product has experienced high rates of default for two main reasons. First, it is almost impossible to properly underwrite cases when the attorney is desperate for money. Regardless of how experienced the underwriting team or how honed the methodology, attorneys will always know a great deal more about their own cases than any third party and, when financially distressed, may engage in hyperbole and obfuscation to get the deal done. Because contingent deals often focus on baskets of cases, rather than the firm's entire portfolio, lawsuit investors unknowingly receive some of the firm's riskiest cases as part of the package, with adverse selection wreaking havoc on the unsuspecting investor.

Second, little emphasis is generally placed on managing counter-party risk, because attorney clients are presumed trustworthy by funding companies as a result of their vocation. However, this assumption—while perhaps true in a general sense—is flawed when considering that subprime attorneys are perhaps the worst equipped of any manager to properly run their businesses and, conversely, the best equipped to avoid payment due to their legal expertise.

Most funding companies have paid the price precisely for these reasons. Rather than structure deals that require the attorneys' fees to be paid into escrow, administered by a third party, or paid by defendant directly to the funding company, they entrusted the attorney to collect and make payment to them. Unfortunately, many attorneys simply did not pay and then used their consider-able litigation experience to frustrate collection efforts. Since these types of attorneys tend to already have bad credit, judgments and other financial issues, reputational risk is usually of little concern for them. In fact, many of the applicants for this type of financing may be facing imminent disbarment.

Others made the mistake of allowing the attorney to pay less than the contractual obligation required upon resolution of the underlying claims, often receiving no replacement claims or significantly worse cases as substitutes, with only minimal follow-up underwriting on these new cases. In many instances, the good cases were eventually replaced by very risky ones that resulted in no recovery.

My experience in this space has not been favorable either. Many of these insights and observations have come from firsthand efforts in structuring and collecting on attorney contingency deals across the country. For these reasons, this product is appropriate for only very adventurous, thick-skinned lawsuit investors—those with a capacity to engage in protracted collection efforts.

Even though it is possible to structure more secure contingent deals with law firms, primarily by increasing the levels of disclosure, evaluating counterparty risk, increasing compliance and other post-investment activity, as well as requiring third-party payment agents, the reality is that few attorneys would agree to participate in such deals or qualify for them.

Another contingent funding tool that has become available to law firms, albeit in limited supply, is appeal funding. Consider a firm that after three years of intensive litigation successfully represented a seriously injured client to a jury verdict—perhaps a judgment of several million dollars. If the losing defendant files for an appeal, it may take years to receive a final adjudication of the matter—presuming the case is not reversed, dismissed, or remanded for a new trial.

There are few specialist funding firms in this area. Some of the same firms that offer tort advances to plaintiffs and contingency loans to attorneys also provide appeal funding. Two notable exceptions are Trial & Appellate Resources and Appeal Funding Partners.

In many respects, appeal funding is similar to the contingency advance for law firms, the critical difference being that there is already a judgment and each deal usually focuses on one case, rather than a basket of cases. In a typical transaction, the funding company will advance an amount to the attorney in return for a stake in the proceeds of the successful appeal. The prevailing rate is two times the investment amount, although much higher rates have been seen in the industry.

This legal finance product shares many of the risks that contingency deals have and it is critical to properly underwrite both the merits of the claims, as well as the counterparty risk inherent in the transaction. Because deals typically focus on only one case, many transactions require that payment is made by the defendant directly to the funding company. This mitigates the problem of non-payment that has frustrated investors in contingency advances.

Even though the majority of cases are affirmed on appeal, as with other contingency law firm deals, it is almost never transparent what actually motivates the attorney to receive appeal funding for a particular case. It could be that the case is a high risk candidate for reversal, dismissal or some other negative event.

However, judgments on appeal present further complications. The same attorney who represented the plaintiff at the trial level frequently handles the appeal, despite the fact that the appeals process merits a specialist practitioner in most situations. Appellate decisions are not made by a jury but a panel of judges who are focused, for the most part, on errors that may have occurred at trial rather than on examining new evidence. For this reason, appellate analysis is usually quite narrow, applying a standard of review that only specialists know well.

At the same time, funding companies that specialize in other legal finance products cannot adequately evaluate this risk because their underwriting staff is not usually comprised of appellate specialists. My personal experience in this space has been similar to other contingent law firm advances, and this is an investment from which I typically refrain. My discussions with colleagues in the industry suggest that most companies are extremely selective about appellate funding.

In the last five years, a new loan product specifically designed for contingency practices has gained popularity among law firms. The broad availability of capital prior to 2008 gave rise to the law firm loan, which is secured by the firm's portfolio of contingency cases. As with tort advances in the mid-nineties, Joe DiNardo also saw an opportunity in funding law firms that were traditionally underbanked by mainstream financial institutions. To address this market, after retiring from practicing law he created a specialty lending company—Counsel Financial—which quickly popularized the law firm line of credit. As financial institutions searched for new, profitable investments, they found that law firms were a receptive audience, as this was one of the few industries for which financing was not yet readily available. Like investments in commercial litigation, law firm loans offer an attractive yield to investors in a scalable, non-correlated product.

The law firm loan pioneered by Counsel Financial is usually a four-year finance package, which combines a revolving line of credit in the first two years, with a term loan for the last two. Law firms make interest-only payments for the line of credit in the first two years, but must also start paying off some principal if they receive certain amounts in fees from settled cases. For the last two years, the firms pay principal and interest. Borrowers can prepay the entire amount sooner without incurring pre-payment penalties, and most deals do not assess a fee for any unused portions of credit lines.

Most lawsuit lenders structure transactions as loans that are repaid from revenues, typically from winning or settling cases. There are about a half-dozen companies that claim to make loans to law firms. Some of the leaders in this niche include companies such as Counsel Financial (formerly related to Plaintiff Support Services), Esquire Bank (an affiliate of LawCash), and Advocate Capital.

Over 250 law firms in New York alone have borrowed money from legal finance firms, often repeatedly.[20] For the largest of these firms, Counsel Financial, the average loan is $1.5 million, but can be as high as $25 million. According to DiNardo, Counsel has loaned approximately $600 million since inception, with approximately $270 million in loans outstanding today. The industry's outstanding investments in law firm loans total more than $500 million when adjusted for interest, finance and penalty charges.[21] Counsel's typical interest rate is 18 percent, with the industry's average rates ranging between 14 and 30 percent.[22]

The primary underwriting involves an evaluation of the firm's total portfolio of cases, which could generally include most tort cases, including motor vehicle, premises, medical malpractice, product liability, and others. In their analysis, funding companies will only consider the value of actual damages being sought, and will not give credit for any potential fees resulting from punitive damages. Providers will also review the firm's financials and will require personal guarantees from the partners, although the core underwriting is based on the value and strength of the underlying case collateral. The loan proceeds can be used for any business purpose, including case expenses, expert witnesses, overhead, salaries, and advertising.

Within the general niche of law firm loans, other firms focus on more narrow types of funding. For example, RD Legal Funding specializes in accelerating contingent fees on settled cases by providing up-front payments to attorneys at a discount in exchange for the right to collect their fees. Daniels Capital also accelerates payments of attorneys' fees, but for criminal defense attorneys who handle indigent clients and receive reimbursement from either the state or federal government.

The financing tool provided by these specialty lenders offers many benefits to the contingency law firm. Because most legal finance companies are operated by attorneys or finance professionals who deal with the legal profession every day, they have become accustomed to the nuances of law firm business models and are proficient at valuing their assets. For this reason, law firms like Anne and David's can qualify for a loan with a legal finance provider more easily than with a traditional lender. Moreover, these specialty loans tend to be much larger than a bank could provide under the same circumstances.

This type of financing can unlock significant capital that would otherwise remain unproductive. If used correctly, the loan proceeds can be used in many ways to increase the franchise value of the firm. For example, partners like Anne and David can free up capital to retain better experts and develop cases more aggressively, increasing their recoveries. They can pursue promising new cases within their practice area where their fees will more than make up for the high interest rate. Firms can also expand into other practice areas and begin accepting cases on contingency. They can hire staff, including attorneys, paralegals, and marketing directors. They can upgrade their office technology and office space.

At the same time, however, the high interest rates are nothing to take lightly. Many law firms lack clear business plans for what they would like to achieve—they simply know that the firm needs money—they may not even be sure how much or how they plan to repay it. As the interest continues to accrue over time, minor miscalculations about how quickly cases will settle, case expenses, or the profitability of marketing campaigns can result in a vicious cycle of debt that may significantly impact the firm.

For this reason, despite early successes in originating a large number of loans, the law firm loan business has slowed significantly since the 2008 financial crisis. As with contingency deals, the initial wave of financing has been wrought with problems as a result of improper deal structuring, cavalier underwriting, and debt mismanagement by borrower attorneys.

In recent years, a significant number of loans defaulted, becoming work-out situations for their investors. For example, the Masry & Vititoe firm of Erin Brockovich fame filed for bankruptcy in 2009 after Edward Masry died. Counsel Financial was a large lender to the Masry firm.

Yet Counsel Financial is not the only company to suffer losses in law firm loans. Stillwater Capital Partners, a hedge fund that reportedly made more than $100 million in law firm loans, was forced to close in early 2011 as a result of investor redemptions. The *New York Times* reported in 2010 that the firm loaned more than $3.5 million to Houston law firm Woodfill & Pressler to finance a large case brought by residents of Somerville, Texas, against BNSF Railway—which the firm ultimately lost.[23]

In fact, many of the companies that offered loan products to attorneys no longer exist or have stopped making new loans, usually because they experienced credit problems from bad loans or because their funding sources collapsed during the crisis. Some examples include Themis Capital and the LawFinance Group. Oasis and Peachtree used to offer attorney funding, though now this service is no longer advertised on their websites.

One of the primary reasons many of these deals became problematic is the same reason why this type of financing is in high demand by attorneys—the underwriting often focuses on the quality of the underlying cases rather than the firms' revenue or balance sheets. This type of due diligence ignores the fact that attorneys are notoriously bad at managing their businesses and their own money. They went to law school to study law, not accounting, finance, or marketing, and many are poorly equipped to run a business. As a result, many borrow more than their revenues allow them to pay back, creating a situation where they are personally responsible for large loans often used to fund expected short-term gains that never materialize.

Also, as with contingency deals, another reason exacerbating default rates in this niche is the nature of the borrower. Lawyers may not be savvy businessmen, but they certainly know their rights and are not timid about enforcing them. For this reason, collecting against attorneys is often an expensive and time-consuming endeavor.

Despite these considerations, even defaulting deals can have a great deal of value, provided the investment company employs an effective compliance and collections strategy. Unlike contingency deals, most loans to lawyers have personal guarantees, and the collateral covers all the assets of the firm, often in perpetuity. Even if a law firm defaults because of a current inability to pay or an act of malfeasance, its cases may still result in future income if the practice endures.

Because of personal guarantees, the attorney is personally liable for the loan amount and must repay it from future assets or income. Therefore, unless the defaulting attorneys decide to switch professions—which will not excuse their obligation—they will always have new cases that will result in future fees, constituting a revenue stream on which the funding company can collect. Unlike contingency transactions, most attorneys who borrow against their cases take reputational risk very seriously.

As the capital markets recover after the 2008 crisis, this product will likely become increasingly available to law firms once again, albeit under more stringent terms. Current deals place a much greater emphasis on the firm's revenue and ability to pay on a current basis, rather than deferring payment as with previous arrangements. With proper mechanisms in place, this product can provide attractive returns to investors, while offering law firms the ability to significantly expand their business models.

CHAPTER 4

THE INVESTMENT PROCESS

Funders seeking to avoid the pitfalls of lawsuit investment must understand the considerations involved in initiating, vetting, executing, and monitoring these types of investments. The more informed the participants, the less likely unpleasant surprises will be down the road—and the more likely that all parties will achieve the underlying goals that gave rise to the lawsuit investment in the first place.

The process of investing in lawsuits is admittedly—and by necessity—complex. Case origination alone encompasses the use of multiple marketing channels to cultivate deals, attorney referrals, and brokers. Funding companies collect basic information about claims and explain its terms to applicants. After the initial vetting process, a more comprehensive review begins to determine eligibility, with relevant documents thoroughly reviewed by dedicated underwriters. Those underwriters have many tools at their disposal to aid in the evaluation process, ranging in complexity from databases to conversations with attorneys and legal experts. Underwriting is a critical step in investing in lawsuits in order to ensure that funders receive the return they expect, and that a myriad of potential problems are avoided. Determining standards for the kind of case, its legal merit, the size of investment, type of attorney compensation, and even jurisdictional and procedural concerns all factor into an investment company's underwriting methodology. The plaintiff's attributes, such as his or her level of engagement, command of the subject matter, and willingness to cooperate, along with the defendant's characteristics, such as their litigation style and ability to pay, will also determine the level of risk entailed by investment in a particular lawsuit. Scrutiny of exhaustive breadth and detail—which this chapter explores—is vital to ensure that lawsuit investments attain the returns they set out to achieve.

Once underwriting is completed, the structuring of the transaction begins. That structure centers on the investment agreement, which sets forth the rights and obligations of investors, plaintiffs, and their attorneys, budgeting, payment arrangements, interclaimant provisions, and other nuances that arise in the course of the investment process. The challenge posed in drafting effective investment agreements lies in striking a balance between the enforceability and flexibility of the document while keeping its terms attractive to clients and attorneys.

The investment process continues even after the consummation of a funding transaction. Providers and their compliance teams must exercise vigilance in managing their investments for the entire life of the claim. Considerations must be made with regard to discount requests, the priority of liens, attorney substitutions, or, at worst, situations that can lead to the complete write-off of an investment. Those investments that avoid a total write-off situation will require payments monitoring, or, in cases of default, collection and dispute resolution. A successful investment process accordingly entails thorough preparation, an investment agreement that accounts for a myriad of contingencies while remaining attractive and easy to understand, as well as continuing oversight of all aspects of the lawsuit and related obligations.

Parties Involved in Legal Finance

Participants in legal finance transactions include recipients, providers, brokers, and lawyers and law firms.

Recipients

There are several types of recipients that typically benefit from legal finance products. They include plaintiffs, law firms, or sometimes even defendants (see Chapter 8 for a more detailed discussion of defendant funding). Plaintiffs are the most common recipients of legal finance. They may be involved in personal injury claims and require funding for living expenses. They may be individuals or companies involved in business disputes that need to fund working capital or litigation expenses. Recipients can also be individuals involved in divorce proceedings or inheritance matters who are not necessarily plaintiffs. Other recipients can include lawyers: solo practitioners or law firms that require non-recourse investments for some of the cases they are handling or conventional loan products against the proceeds of all their cases.

Providers

Providers are funding companies or private investors that—for a fee—will purchase portions of future proceeds from litigation for an upfront cash payment or commit to paying for the expenses of a lawsuit for a stake in its outcome. Providers might fund living expenses if they are making consumer lawsuit advances, or litigation expenses if they specialize in funding commercial claims. Some are lenders providing loans to attorneys and law firms. Providers also purchase patents and judgments directly.

Brokers

Legal finance brokers originate and arrange transactions between providers and recipients, playing a significant role in expanding legal finance origination while providing value to both funders and recipients. The majority of websites advertising legal finance products are in fact brokers who refer their leads to providers.

Lawyers and Law Firms

Attorneys and law firms are cornerstones of the investment process. They enable lawsuits to proceed by educating plaintiffs about their rights while collecting and developing evidence for trial. They manage the plaintiffs' understanding of their claims, their performance and expectations. Lawyers may advise their clients about legal strategy, where to seek medical treatment, and usually review the lawsuit funding contract as well. They are important sources of origination, referring many clients to funding companies. Attorneys also facilitate the underwriting process by providing investors with critical information about claims so they may assess their prospects. After investments are made, they update funders regarding the development of their cases. In most claims, attorneys serve as custodians of funds for all of the lawsuit's stakeholders and distribute those funds to them in an equitable manner. As a result, they have significant influence over the outcome of cases and investors' returns. Put simply, legal finance transactions cannot happen without their involvement. It is critical that funders become adept in managing their relationships with attorneys.

Origination

Investments in lawsuits are not yet mainstream financial products. They are not very common or liquid. They are also not easily transferrable, insofar as they are almost always attached to a servicer. One can neither simply find investment opportunities on an exchange nor acquire them in great numbers. While there have been several portfolio purchases throughout the years, at this point investors must find one-off investment opportunities by directly advertising their services and interacting with prospects that are looking for this kind of funding.

Providers use multiple marketing channels to originate their deals. Tort companies are very active in retail advertising and maintain a ubiquitous presence on television and the Internet, where thousands of websites promote the product known as lawsuit loans, lawsuit advances, lawsuit funding, and pre-settlement funding. Commercial funding companies and law firm lenders are also active on the Internet, but often find it difficult to distinguish their message from the background noise of tort advertising saturating the web in recent years. Many companies in the industry refer business to one another, as they may have different specialties.

Attorney referrals are an important source of business and providers are very active in getting their message out to the legal community. Tort advance firms and law firm lenders target mostly personal injury firms, while commercial funders focus on business litigation firms. Many of the funders advertise in legal periodicals, sponsor events and legal education seminars, or attend attorney conventions and legal industry trade shows. The legal community has mixed feelings about the industry but in recent years has grown more comfortable with it, especially with respect to commercial funding and law firm lending. Many lawyers have heard about the emergence of legal finance, but the majority still has no direct experience with this type of financing. Greater acceptance from attorneys will drive the expansion of this industry in the coming years.

Brokers are an important part of many providers' deal origination. Plaintiffs and providers have used investment brokers since the early days of the industry. Innovations in advertising techniques have allowed brokers to compete with funding companies—who have never been particularly efficient in originating cases—on a level playing field.

They have become a feature of the investment process because they increase funding volume and lend predictability to origination costs. For example, new providers may not have the same access to customers as an experienced broker. Some brokers have honed their Internet skills, achieving high organic rankings or becoming adept at pay-per-click advertising. Others have mastered print or TV advertising, while certain brokers have developed key relationships with referral sources like law firms, medical offices, accountants and investment firms.

Brokers offer certain advantages to plaintiffs as well. They can furnish considerable market information regarding prices, products and market conditions. They know their industry and have already established relations with eager funding sources. They can often refer their prospects to multiple sources that can provide the most capital for a particular claim, including cases that are otherwise difficult to fund because of complicating factors. Another benefit of using a broker is cost—they tend to use cheaper providers because lower rates make it is easier for them to close deals.

Many providers will pass broker commissions on to the funding recipient using various structures. Depending on the size of the investment, brokers typically receive a front-end commission ranging from 5 percent to 20 percent of the deal for the referral, and some brokers in commercial cases also receive a small portion of the recovery. In commercial claims, accountants, investment banks, and other consultants often refer clients to funding companies, but they are not always compensated for it.

A broker's interaction with the market profoundly affects the provider with whom the broker associates. Common problems include situations where brokers misrepresent rates or the funding process to their clients. Some may be overly aggressive in contacting prospects and obtaining case documents from law firms. Others will pressure providers to do the deal, sometimes to make much larger investments than the circumstances of cases support. Investors should be very careful in arranging their relationships with investment intermediaries. Many funders conduct background checks on all new brokers while also requiring them to abide by a specific set of best practices.

Underwriting

A typical transaction begins when a plaintiff or attorney applies for funding by contacting a provider, usually after finding a funding company online, seeing an ad, or being referred by an attorney or broker. The funding company will collect basic information about the claim and will explain its terms to the applicant. At this stage, after interviewing the applicant, the funder may request to see documents to make a preliminary determination. Applicants who do not meet the provider's investment criteria are notified of the rejection. Plaintiffs who are pre-approved for further evaluation are also notified and their attorney is contacted to provide case documents. The plaintiff must provide authorization to his or her attorney to disclose the case records to the provider. Once the documents are received, they are forwarded to the underwriting department for a more thorough review.

As with other financial industries, the fortunes of lawsuit investors rise and fall with their investment decisions. Funders must pick winners over losers, and, at the end of the day, they must also get paid. Lawsuits are uncertain by their very nature, and bringing a successful claim is no easy undertaking. Many disputes have nuanced arguments on both sides, while investors have only limited information to make their funding decisions. At the same time, because lawsuit investments can span a number of years, an intervening number of risks can arise to frustrate a funder's ability to earn a return on its investment.

Even when legal finance is swathed with risk, a surprising number of people wrongly assume that lawsuits are safe bets because most cases never reach the verdict stage. They assert that most cases settle out of court and cite various studies confirming that the overwhelming majority of all claims never reach a jury.

This is misleading.

The statistics confirming a bias toward settlement versus trial could contribute to the mistaken conclusion that plaintiffs almost always get paid. Instead, many cases never see a jury because they are dismissed, abandoned, or voluntarily discontinued. As previously noted, most lawsuits that do settle are resolved for only a fraction of the plaintiff's demand. Post-settlement problems can also arise because defendants frequently default on their settlement agreements.

Investments in lawsuits that do not resolve as expected share some common problems. In many claims, facts come to light during discovery that can negatively impact the case. New case law may invalidate a claim's legal basis. Witnesses may fare poorly in depositions. Clients can disappear or die. Cases can be dismissed for many reasons. In tort claims, attorneys routinely withdraw from representation, leaving the plaintiff (or the investors) scrambling to find replacement counsel. Lawyers can fail to pursue seemingly great cases, sitting on them for years with no apparent reason. In commercial disputes, particularly contract claims, unexpected counterclaims can devastate compelling cases. Plaintiffs might agree to accept "in kind" settlements, without any cash component to pay their investors. Defendants may play shell games with their assets or file for bankruptcy, making them judgment proof. Lawyers could make mistakes or get into trouble. Many lawsuits simply run out of money, significantly reducing the value of the claim. Even if a jury decides a damage award in favor of the plaintiff, the court can still lower the amount if it deems the award excessive.

In reality, investors face a myriad of risks that could reduce their returns, render their investments worthless, or even expose them to unexpected liability. The additional layers of counter-party risk and the potential for court interference after the fact add further complexity to funding transactions in this field. Legal claims entail complex underwriting because they are subject to numerous idiosyncrasies, any of which could significantly impair their value and collectability. The underwriting process attempts to prognosticate an outcome using only a snapshot of the lawsuit in time, even though massive momentum swings commonly occur in litigation, potentially altering the balance of power.

Plaintiffs and their attorneys inevitably know much more about their claims than outsiders looking in. What if a plaintiff's decision to seek funding is motivated by an expectation of a negative outcome? To minimize the risk of adverse selection, investors need an effective case selection methodology to help choose suitable opportunities with only a sample of lawsuit data. This is also true for investors who provide lines of credit to law firms since understanding the prospects of lawsuits is an integral part of valuing their collateral. The underwriting process—the method of critically analyzing investments to select desirable opportunities—goes beyond evaluating the merits of underlying claims. It comprehensively assesses the investment opportunity by considering extrinsic factors affecting the prospects for a favorable recovery, while also mitigating significant counterparty risks that can arise from both clients and their attorneys.

Funders generally employ similar techniques in evaluating investments. Many of the issues that determine the prospects of lawsuits are rooted in common sense, while others tend to be highly technical, requiring specialized knowledge and experience.

The underwriting methodology largely depends on the funder's specialization. Tort advance companies will mostly underwrite personal injury cases, whereas commercial funders are adept at evaluating business disputes. Legal finance lenders underwrite attorneys and law firms for their suitability as borrowers for lines of credit. The first two methodologies are fairly similar, except that average commercial claims are typically far more complex than average tort cases, requiring a much deeper dive into every aspect of litigation. Companies that provide lines of credit to law firms, on the other hand, also require a credit evaluation of the borrowers as part of the investment process, which other forms of legal finance products do not.

Funders typically use in-house underwriters with legal backgrounds to review claims. For example, law firm lender Counsel Financial employs a staff of eight underwriters, including former insurance defense attorneys and retired judges.[1] Funders may also outsource underwriting to law firms or companies like LawMax, which specialize in servicing lawsuit investments on behalf of third parties and provide underwriting as part of their services. In rare instances, investors without any formal legal training undertake to evaluate lawsuits themselves which yield a broad range of outcomes depending on the complexity of cases and their experience with similar matters.

Underwriters may use a number of tools to help them in their evaluation process. These include online databases, paid legal resources and computer-assisted legal research services like Bloomberg Law, LexisNexis, VerdictSearch, and Westlaw. Underwriters will also rely on past experience with similar investments, as well as conversations with attorneys and legal experts, to form their investment decisions. Some companies have built proprietary models and applications to help automate the decision making process.

First, most funding companies will vet cases early on in their origination process to exclude opportunities that clearly do not fit their investment strategy by narrowing candidates for additional underwriting.

Second, they will collect and review supporting documentation from the plaintiffs and law firms to help perform a legal and procedural analysis of the claims. Most will discuss cases with plaintiffs' attorneys and then perform research regarding any relevant issues.

Third, they will consider all of the information they collected, including the legal merits, procedural issues, jurisdictional risk, and suitability of the plaintiffs, defendants, and legal teams. They will also consider pricing and return, evaluate counterparty risk and collectability issues, and identify any encumbrances and the order of payments for any return if the case settles.

Finally, the underwriters will arrive at a funding decision by approving, rejecting or postponing the claim for investment, specifying the terms of any approved deal. Some underwriters may also supervise the execution of the investment agreement when the funding offer is accepted by the client. Underwriting times will vary according to case complexity and the size of investment.

After an investment is approved, the funding company will make a one-time payment to the plaintiff, or will agree on a process to make several investments over time, which is known as a *follow-on investment*. In commercial claims, follow-on investments are often made upon the completion of certain litigation milestones or to pay litigation expenses as they become due.

Typical Investment Process for Tort Advances

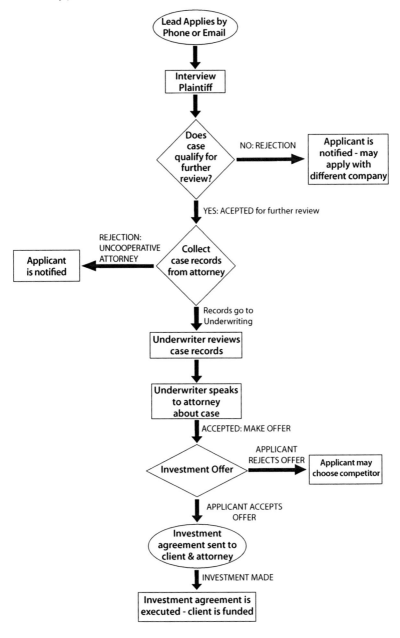

In both consumer and commercial deals, as a condition of agreeing to invest in a case, funders require the client's attorney to meet certain basic obligations. The attorney is required, among other things, to pay the funding company the proceeds of any settlement or verdict before making any payments to the client; to provide periodic updates about the status of the case; to inform the company if he or she is replaced by another attorney; and to inform the company when the case is resolved. The attorney is also required to disclose all previous liens, including prior funding from other investors, before a provider will agree to fund a deal. In commercial transactions, an escrow agent appointed by the funder often takes custody of settlement proceeds and then distributes them according to the investment agreement.

While credit underwriting methodologies of law firm lenders are beyond the scope of this book, it is important to mention that companies in this space will additionally look to evaluate the borrowers' revenues and costs. Lenders will request to see the firms' financials, as well as several years of tax returns from them and their individual partners. They will also look at credit reports to determine the bankability of the borrowers. As a general rule, lawsuit lenders like Counsel Financial will only fund firms involved in personal injury litigation and not commercial claims.[2]

As part of their review, lawsuit lenders will do an in-depth evaluation of the borrower's portfolio: they will verify the existence of legal services retainer agreements between the law firm and its clients; assess past settlement performance for similar claims; and, perhaps most importantly, examine the quality of the cases that make up the portfolio.

Determining Underwriting Standards

Inevitably, investors will originate claims that belie their investment strategy. After all, there are some 20 million civil lawsuits filed every year in state and federal courts around the country. Most of those prospects will be clearly unsuitable, but many will not be so obvious. It is the underwriters' job not only to properly examine investment opportunities, but to do so in an efficient manner.

Every lawsuit is unique. Claims can have very different fact patterns, making it difficult to be a subject matter expert for each type of claim. They also have thousands of pages of court records, evidence and supporting documents, all of which take substantial time to review. Casting too wide a net inundates staff with unproductive activities, while significantly impeding their ability to find good prospects. There is a lot of noise in the industry, making it nearly impossible to review all investment prospects individually without crashing the system. The underwriting methodology needs to be consistent with one's industry experience, available resources, and investment objectives.

Many problems can be avoided by clearly defining the acquisition parameters, which helps companies become more efficient by filtering leads that do not fit their strategy. There is, however, no one-size-fits-all formula. For some smaller or part-time investors, a less formal approach may work well. For professional investors, on the other hand, a highly structured underwriting process is critical to efficiently identify unacceptable risks. The underwriting system should also be smart, allowing the investor to adjust the methodology as they gain experience and learn from their mistakes. As objectives evolve over time, the underwriting policy should undergo revisions to bring it into compliance with those changes.

In addition, vigilant portfolio monitoring is critical to understanding how investments will perform over time. It also provides investors with important data to help evaluate and refine their methodology. Statistical analysis tools for reporting, back-testing, and performance tracking should be implemented across a wide range of parameters, capturing data for categories such as vintage years, investment types, geography, investment amounts, attorneys, and brokers, among others.

What types of claims should an investor fund? The answer varies greatly among lawsuits. Should a funder invest in tort cases, commercial claims, or both? Perhaps they should fund attorneys and law firms? Or maybe consider patent infringement claims? Even if one is skilled at evaluating certain types of cases, that knowledge may not apply to other types of claims. Judgments on appeal, for example, are notoriously difficult to review because they require very narrow knowledge of appellate law and procedure. Similarly, medical malpractice claims involve judgment calls about standards of care, requiring a background in medicine. Patent infringement underwriting may require engineering know-how due to the technical nature of the subject matter. Loans to attorneys require a high level of sophistication and a war chest large enough to accommodate the borrowing needs of many law firms. As a result, many providers have carved out niches in their core competencies, usually specializing in certain types of claims within the larger industry. They have done their homework in their space and are reluctant to consider claims that require any other specialized knowledge to underwrite.

What is the intended use of funds? Claims can be distinguished based on the plaintiffs' required use of funds. In tort claims, for example, investors predominantly advance funds for living expenses since these claims are typically bankrolled by contingency attorneys. In commercial matters, however, the use of funds is not always clear and a combination of factors may drive the demand for capital. When business disputes arise, plaintiffs frequently endure a significant economic impact as a result of defendants' acts or omissions, often leading to financial distress for companies and their owners. At the same time, the litigation process will consume a great deal of their time, usually preventing them from pursuing other endeavors and earning a living. Plaintiffs may be required to pay for the costs of the lawsuit as well as keep their companies operational and their families looked after during this difficult period. Funding companies have different policies regarding the permitted use of funds by litigants.

Should investors make one investment in a case or several over time? Making multiple investments gives the investor significant flexibility in structuring deals, allowing greater control of its exposure by requiring a graduated deployment schedule and giving the funder veto power over any subsequent investments. At the same time, however, multiple investments are both time and capital intensive. If funders make follow-on investments, they will typically implement adequate budgeting, forecasting and cash management systems to help manage cash flow and keep track of their obligations.

Because all cases are unique, the plaintiff's situation is also likely to differ significantly from one case to another. Some consumer deals may require funding a plaintiff in several tranches, either because the case acquires greater value over time, or perhaps to implement financial discipline for the recipient, ensuring appropriate levels of funding are available for personal expenses throughout the entire life of the case. In commercial cases, for example, funding companies commonly set funding milestones like pre-discovery, post-discovery, and jury selection, and apportion their investments based on the plaintiff's progress through the various stages of litigation. Furthermore, unlike pure monetization deals where investments are made in one lump sum, funding commitments to finance litigation expenses frequently require follow-on investments to pay bills as they become due, requiring the continuous re-underwriting of claims.

How is the legal team being compensated for their work? In almost all tort cases, the plaintiff's attorneys work on a contingency basis. In commercial cases, however, the majority of attorneys work on a current pay basis and bill by the hour. The payment arrangements that are part of the legal retainer agreement between the attorney and the plaintiff are a good indicator of whether there is alignment of interests among the parties.

Contingency attorneys often provide the best alignment of interests because they are, in essence, co-investors in the same lawsuit. They must invest their firm's time and resources with only an expectation of a future payment as their incentive, one that greatly depends on their success in litigating cases to a successful resolution. When attorneys pay for some or all of the costs of litigation, investors can draw favorable inferences about the legal team's confidence level. Ostensibly, the greater stake they have in the outcome, the more confident they are about the matters they are undertaking.

However, there is a downside to contingency arrangements. As we have seen in our discussion of attorney funding products, lawyers are not immune from overextending themselves. If the contingency law firm does not have adequate resources to properly finance the litigation, the entire process will be imperiled. It is common for undercapitalized firms in these situations to "wing it," only to cut their losses and push for early settlements far below what was originally expected. To reduce this risk, it is critical to properly vet law firms' financial capabilities to ensure they are properly capitalized to support the claims being considered.

Current pay arrangements may also work for investors who specialize in financing litigation expenses, especially if they desire to significantly scale their deployment of capital. A majority of the marquee, higher stakes commercial cases come from top tier law firms and litigation boutiques, many of which do not accept cases on contingency. In addition, many clients are reluctant to pay high contingent fees, which can exceed 50 percent of the recovery in some cases. Current pay arrangements can be useful in securing top legal talent and a greater share of the recovery for plaintiffs in lawsuits with large damages.

As with contingency arrangements, there are problems with current pay agreements as well. Even if such firms may give investors access to larger, more compelling cases, they can also exact steep hourly fees for their services. Some are happy to collect fat retainers and bill their time without any regard to the outcome of the claim. This revenue expectation can unfortunately engender overstated confidence while in reality masking significant legal and procedural weaknesses, making the underwriter's job even more complicated. This is especially true in the current context of a depressed economy, which has dramatically affected law firm profitability, causing fierce competition for revenue among partners and law firms.

There is also the additional risk that investment will experience cost overruns arising from unforeseen—and often excessive—legal fees. Lawyers are not particularly adept at formulating budgets or expense projections. Current pay arrangements provide no incentives to lawyers to save money and provide little correlation between expenses and legal outcomes. As a result, investors may find themselves in situations where claims have exceeded their funding commitments, requiring them to decide if they should continue funding them further. One way to minimize this risk is by requiring attorneys to commit to a budget for all litigation expenses and cap their own fees once they reach the agreed to maximum. Another approach is to negotiate a flat fee with counsel prior to making any commitment.

What should determine investment minimums or investment limits? The amount of capital plaintiffs seek to raise depends on several factors. It may hinge on how confident or uncertain the plaintiff is about the outcome of the matter. In theory, a higher level of uncertainty should increase the plaintiff's appetite for capital, especially if those funds can be applied toward personal use. It may fall on how much they need to keep their companies afloat or personal emergencies that require immediate capital. The size of the claim, the plaintiffs' financial situation, and the costs of the lawsuit that are not being covered by attorneys are also important drivers of funding demand, which can range between just a few thousand to tens of millions of dollars.

Nevertheless, some deals are just too small to be worthwhile. Consider that lawsuit investments require substantial investments of the investor's time to properly evaluate, particularly when involving complex or technical issues. Post-investment activities also consume bandwidth to varying degrees since one has to stay on top of each matter during the course of litigation, while attending to any follow-on investments, workouts, or disputes that arise. Setting minimum funding amounts can effectively focus an investment strategy. Any opportunity should offer sufficient magnitude to justify the acquisition, underwriting and carrying costs of that investment.

Making investments that are too large is another common problem. Even though investors should be prepared to take significant losses in this business (unsuccessful cases usually result in a total loss), putting too many eggs in a single basket can devastate an entire investment portfolio. Some cases are appropriate only for well-capitalized investors. Internally, we limit any one investment to a maximum of 2 percent of available capital.

In addition to investment limits, investors often fail to account for attorney concentration risk in their underwriting methodology, making them too dependent on the fortunes of one or several law firms. Funding too many lawsuits with one firm or attorney also compromises some of the objectivity that is critical to the underwriting process, providing the undesirable incentive to fund cases on auto-pilot, perhaps out of a false sense of security or fear of rocking the boat with a major business partner.

Which jurisdictions are safe for legal finance? As we shall see, legal precedent relating to investments in lawsuits is very limited in most states. Some states do have laws that are adverse to the legal finance industry, while other states may have licensing or other requirements that make investing in lawsuits opaque, onerous or risky. When investors fund matters in one of these jurisdictions, or if any of the parties are located there, they may have problems collecting even if the case is successful. For this reason, it is important to evaluate the investment jurisdiction of the claim early on in the investment process.

Strength of Legal Merits

Underwriters must first evaluate the strength of a claim's underlying legal merits—the inherent rights and wrongs of the dispute. A case being considered for investment must have a valid basis, setting forth adequate facts from which the court could find a valid claim, such as a denial of an existing legal right like patent infringement. The plaintiffs' court documents will cite legal authorities, including statutory and case law to support their arguments.

Generally, claims that are accepted for funding are based on widely accepted legal theories or causes of action. These include, among others, contract-based actions; fraud; breach of fiduciary duty; torts such as assault, battery, invasion of privacy, fraud, slander, negligence, intentional infliction of emotional distress; and statutory causes of action such as violations of state and federal laws concerning trade secrets, unfair competition, RICO, labor and employment and intellectual property rights.

To prevail, plaintiffs *must prove certain elements of their causes of action.* For example, in claims of negligence, the elements are: the existence of a duty; breach of that duty; proximate cause by that breach; and damages. In breach of contract claims, however, plaintiffs must prove different elements, including: the existence of a valid contract; that defendant breached that contract; that plaintiff performed all obligations to the contract prior to filing the claim; that plaintiff notified defendant about the breach; and that plaintiff sustained damages as a result of that breach.

Underwriters must determine if plaintiffs have a high probability of winning with their particular facts. This analysis serves as the basis of the underwriting process. A claim must be founded on well-established legal grounds, which sets forth a tight nexus between the alleged facts and prevailing law. For example, in torts claims, a party must have been negligent or intentionally wrongful, and that party must have caused the injury. In breach of contract cases, however, there must be a valid contact among the parties, one with an offer and acceptance, as well as a breach of obligations under that contract.

Complaints, motions, briefs, mediation memoranda and other court documents establish the various causes of action on which the claim relies. Underwriters know which documents they want to see and will typically send a case questionnaire to the law firm. They may also have a discussion with the attorney about the facts and circumstances of the dispute. In legal claims that have not yet been filed in court, court records will be unavailable. In these instances, attorney correspondence rather than court documents set forth the causes of action and relief their clients are seeking.

Underwriters also examine evidence to corroborate the allegations contained in the court documents, as well as review any defenses or counterclaims that are interposed by defendants. They may examine medical reports, invoices, correspondence, or expert witness statements to decide if plaintiffs have enough proof to substantiate their cases.

Procedural Matters

Compelling legal merits are not the only critical components of successful claims. Legal procedure is just as important to the outcome of litigation because cases are often decided on technical grounds. Clients and attorneys who are unfamiliar with procedural rules may inadvertently violate requirements that have nothing to do with the merits, and as a result devastate their claim. Even after successful verdicts, a large number of cases are overturned on procedural technicalities. Good attorneys can skillfully navigate this procedural maze to achieve a stalemate or other undesirable results for their adversaries. For this reason, it is critical to have an accurate overview of the claim's procedural history, as well as an understanding of how future procedural issues will affect the claim at hand.

The corresponding analysis can be fairly involved.

As mentioned, the U.S. legal system is designed to be adversarial rather than inquisitorial. Attorneys are given wide latitude to control both the preparation and presentation of their cases, much more so than their brethren in other countries. The rules of civil procedure have been developed to help guide and encourage attorneys to develop, manage, and ultimately settle cases with limited judicial supervision. In many respects, these rules are designed to dispose of cases, or parts of cases, without having them decided by juries.

Procedural law comprises the rules by which courts determine what happens in lawsuits, administrative proceedings or arbitrations. Procedural rules typically impose specific time limitations upon the parties that may either accelerate or (more commonly) slow down the pace of proceedings. At the core of these procedures is a broad discovery system that allows each side access to the other's documents and witnesses for trial preparation. During this process, litigants constantly adjust strategies in response to new information that comes to light, which may either strengthen or weaken their cases. For this reason, attorneys require knowledge and skill to manage the discovery process in a manner most advantageous to their client.

In addition, the duopoly of federal and state courts often allows a case to be tried in one or more courts. This adds the further complexity of overlapping jurisdictions, which requires a procedural framework to govern the apportionment of cases to the various courts. The selection of the forum where the trial will take place may offer a number of strategic advantages to one or the other side. For example, some jurisdictions may offer more favorable case law. Some courts may be more sophisticated in resolving complex commercial claims, while others may have a reputation for specific outcomes when deciding tort cases. A particular jurisdiction may have a sympathetic jury pool that may be prejudicial to the interests of the plaintiff or defendant. Some courts move their case loads faster than others, while others are notorious for their bottlenecks. Because of the perceived advantages of having cases heard in specific forums, litigants often maneuver to exploit these procedural rules to gain the upper hand.

Underwriters must, therefore, pay close attention to procedural issues, especially in more complex cases. The procedural record and schedules are often available by examining case files, and in limited circumstances, online via Bloomberg Law, LexisNexis, Pacer, Westlaw, and a growing number of state courts' websites. Conversations with the client and the client's attorney can also be helpful in crystallizing procedural weaknesses, as well as identifying key milestones that will affect the outcome of the claim. Case files containing the procedural history are also available to the public from the court clerk. In many cases, underwriters can simply ask for the file in person or request the procedural history and case status by phone.

In some circumstances, underwriters may decide to postpone the making of an investment due to impending procedural events, such as motions to dismiss, or motions for summary judgment, which may lead to dismissal of the claim early in the process. It is generally a good idea to wait until these motions are decided in the client's favor before investing. If the defendant's motions are denied, the case acquires greater legitimacy in the eyes of the litigants, as the plaintiff's chances of an early exit are reduced and the prospects of a settlement increase as pressure builds for the defendant to resolve the claim prior to an uncertain and potentially disastrous verdict.

The Plaintiff

Plaintiffs play a major role in determining case outcomes. Litigation is a demanding experience, requiring great determination and organizational skill. This is especially true in commercial litigation, where the plaintiff must adapt to an ever-changing legal landscape while concurrently marshaling multiple resources. At the same time, the plaintiff must also figure out how to finance the entire undertaking, including his own expenses.

Not everyone is up to this task.

Some lack the skill or enthusiasm needed to bring disputes to their final conclusion, even when a lot of money is at stake. Others may not have the time to give testimony or meet with attorneys and experts. Plaintiffs may not be able to clearly articulate their position in court. There may be problems with their background that make their testimony unreliable. There may be issues with their appearance or demeanor, which, again, may cast negative inferences.

Plaintiffs are the primary witnesses in many cases. Underwriters must therefore assess whether they will make sympathetic witnesses. Strong facts are not enough—credibility is essential. The witness must have the capacity to make a good impression on a judge or a jury since the amount of time they will spend together is very limited.

As a witness, the plaintiff must be intelligent enough to understand legal theories and to withstand a cross-examination, which often requires intimate command of the lawsuit's details. Determining how good a witness the plaintiff will be is one of the most critical assessments one will make when evaluating new cases for funding.

Many funders will conduct background checks to pick up any problems with credibility or potential threats of fraud. Underwriters will also ask attorneys to provide as much detail as possible regarding their clients. Is the client likeable? Is the client litigious? How would the attorney rate this client as a witness? Does the client get along with the legal team? Does the client have reasonable expectations about the outcome of his or her case? Plaintiffs with extensive criminal records, troubled backgrounds, and immigration problems are just some examples of high-risk categories.

The Defendants

An accurate assessment of defendants is just as essential to the underwriting process as evaluating plaintiffs. Defendants have different characteristics and personalities. They can be individuals, businesses, municipalities or governments. They can be foreign or domestic. They can be paragons of their industry or notorious miscreants. Some defendants are very rich while others have few assets or are judgment proof. It is the underwriters' job to consider the circumstances of defendants' involvement in claims and make assumptions about their capabilities and motivation to resolve disputes.

The defendants' identities and litigation histories are very useful in forecasting their behavior. Are they one-time litigants or repeat players who are sued regularly for similar or different issues? Since litigation is usually a matter of public record, many one-time defendants are sensitive about their image and compelled to resolve bona fide claims against them expeditiously. Conversely, many defendants such as banks, insurance companies and manufacturers of dangerous products are repeat players who are sued frequently. They are less preoccupied about their image and more concerned with their vulnerability to future lawsuits. Such defendants have developed sophisticated litigation techniques designed to mitigate liability and deter future litigation.

Are they more prone to settle, or do they fight to the end? Even repeat players may have different approaches to managing their liability. For example, some insurance companies prefer to settle cases before they are filed in court, while others will not make any offers, at least not until the claim is near its trial date. As recurrent defendants usually have reputations for adopting particular litigation strategies, underwriters will research previous outcomes to understand how defendants have handled similar disputes in the past.

Ability to Pay and Collection Risk

All of the elements of a claim may be very compelling, but what if the defendant has no money to pay an award or settlement? Or what if the defendant is rich, but his assets are hidden in offshore bank accounts? In disputes over money, there is always a risk that the winner will not be able to collect from the loser.

Do defendants have enough money to pay damages? At the outset, it may be clear that defendant lacks the assets necessary to satisfy a judgment, which would make litigation impractical. Collection risks, however, can arise down the road as well. Until the plaintiff is paid or is able to levy on a judgment, he bears the risk of a hollow victory if the defendant shields or spends its assets during the course of litigation.

The defendant's financial condition will often determine their ability to pay. Well-capitalized defendants are certainly in a better position to pay damages than poorer ones. A defendant may simply not have enough assets to satisfy a judgment or even interpose a compelling settlement offer. Therefore, the defendants' ability to pay damages—and the relative certainty of that payout—is one of the most important underwriting considerations when evaluating any case. It should be addressed early on in the underwriting process.

So why would someone bring a case where the defendant's ability to pay is questionable? There are several reasons. Collection problems are not generally indicative of a claim's underlying legal merits and many lawyers are happy work on them if they are being paid. For example, contract disputes are some of the most common commercial claims, accounting for the majority of non-tort litigation in both state and federal court. In many cases, the underlying legal merits of contract disputes are quite clear: there is a legitimate contract and one party has breached it. Despite this, many contract claims are in fact collection efforts as plaintiffs attempt to compel payment by finding, seizing and liquidating assets. If plaintiffs believe they will be successful in locating and seizing assets, they may decide to undertake the endeavor. Plaintiffs, however, are not always able to properly assess this risk, especially when bringing lawsuits for emotional rather than economic motivations.

In reality, these types of claims frequently go nowhere. Lawsuits may run out of money long before the defendant is ever compelled to pay. Attorneys could lose interest and drag their feet or withdraw from representation entirely. Defendants might move to different jurisdictions, file for bankruptcy, or reorganize their businesses. They can hide their assets or enter into settlement agreements which they fail to honor. Other creditors or lien holders like the IRS may have priority to any proceeds. Some collection cases do settle, but the uncertainty relating to the timing and eventuality of payment complicate the underwriting process significantly.

Are financial records available? If the defendant is a large company, its finances are either publically available or discoverable though business data providers. In cases against individuals, some financial information can be obtained by looking at public records, including real estate records; any past lawsuits or judgments; bankruptcies; UCC liens, or other information. A simple Internet search can yield remarkable amounts of useful data.

How will such a payment impact the defendant? In some circumstances, a defendant may have enough money to satisfy a judgment, but the prospect of such a payment may devastate its finances and future prospects well before any final decision is handed down by the court. Public companies, for example, can see their stock price drop precipitously in the event of a serious lawsuit against them. Threats to a company's very existence can lead to desperate reactions like filing for bankruptcy or arranging asset sales, further complicating the collection process and significantly delaying the recovery. Underwriters should be careful to evaluate the reasonableness of recovery expectations against the true capacity of defendants to pay those amounts.

Is the ultimate award enforceable? Even if defendants have sufficient resources, can they legally be compelled to pay? If defendants or their assets are located where the plaintiff cannot reach them, any judgment may be uncollectable. For this reason, claims against foreign defendants can be an enormous challenge. In addition, defendants who are individuals are greater collection risks because they typically have fewer assets. They may also have a greater capacity to secrete their assets or frustrate the collection process. Unlike businesses and government entities, they may move around, change bank accounts, or transfer their assets to trusts and nominees. In these situations, even if plaintiffs are entitled to punitive relief as a result of defendants' bad faith, the practicalities of litigation will make this very difficult and expensive.

Insurance

Is the defendant insured? The availability of insurance strongly indicates a defendant's ability to pay. Insurance plays an integral role in most civil claims, with issues like policy coverage, determinations of fault, and the calculation of compensation forming the core of providers' concerns. It is comparatively more relevant in tort claims than in commercial matters because most people and businesses are required by law to have insurance to cover liability arising from negligent acts. The typical example is car insurance. All developed countries require motorists to be insured. Another example is homeowner's insurance, which may protect against fire damage or even accidents in the swimming pool. Most defendants in commercial claims, on the other hand, are not covered by insurance for business disputes such as breach of contract. Instead, they are directly responsible for paying any damages assessed against them. Exceptions to this rule abound, however, since almost any loss or liability is insurable at some price.

An insurance claim—which begins before a lawsuit is filed—occurs when a party is injured, whether physically, economically or both, and then seeks payment from the defendant or the defendant's insurance carrier. A series of intermediate steps must occur before payment is actually made to the claimant—if at all. Potential conflicts may arise when both sides calculate disparate compensation models, working from different views of what is appropriate under the circumstances. Essentially, claimants seek the maximum payment from the insurance provider, while the carrier uses its best efforts to minimize any payment to the claimant. This tension leads to complications and, potentially, litigation.

Due to the variability intrinsic to this branch of law, insurance policies, particularly those involving personal injury claims, are quite diverse. Insurance providers may have to compensate victims for medical care, lost income, disabilities arising from the accident, emotional damages, and lost property. Additionally, insurers cover car owners, homeowners, businesses and working professionals, all of whom require different types and amounts of coverage.

Insurance policies are contracts. Like all contracts, they can be written to cover almost anything. Not only does insurance exist for different kinds of vehicles—motorcycles, cars, tractor-trailers, etc.—but policies can be individualized to cover as much, or as little, as the policy holder desires. Still, the wide variety of insurance policies share some commonalities.

Almost all claims require at least three determinations by the insurance provider. First, the insurance provider determines what the insurance policy actually covers. Second, the provider determines fault with regard to the relevant incident. Third, the carrier arrives at a formulaic approach to calculate a compensation amount to begin negotiations with the claimant. Understanding the manner in which insurance providers make these determinations is therefore critical to grasping how payments are made.

When a claim is filed, the carrier will review the scope of the insured's policy. The insured does not necessarily have to be the purchaser of the insurance policy. For example, dependents and, in some cases, guests are also covered. In addition, third-party participants also qualify to collect from the insured's provider. This is known as *third-party coverage*, or *liability insurance*, which covers costs incurred by individuals other than the insured. This is always the first step because the carrier's subsequent decisions will differ depending on whether the payment is to the insured or a third party.

◆ Determining Compensation

Insurance adjusters are employed by insurance providers to make determinations regarding incidents and to decide who is at fault. The adjuster will discuss the incident with the parties involved, refer to documents like police and incident reports, and then try to determine the distinct levels of fault with regard to those parties. There is no exact science or formula to this process, as each jurisdiction has precedent which guides the adjuster's decisions.

The adjuster will be guided by the same reasoning as a court in that state. When a damages claim is filed with a court, the person who is found to have caused the accident typically pays for the resulting damage. If more than one person caused the damage, then negligence is distributed among the parties based on state apportionment laws. Four systems are used in establishing damage awards throughout the United States. They include *pure contributory negligence, pure comparative negligence, modified comparative negligence* (50 percent bar rule), and *modified comparative negligence* (51 percent bar rule).[3] Depending on the jurisdiction, this allocation will directly impact the damages awarded. For instance, the fact finder may determine that the defendant, the plaintiff, or both, caused the accident. Based on the evidence presented, the judge or jury will then allocate the amount that each party was negligent.

◆ Calculating Damages and Settlement

What damages did the claimant suffer as a result of the incident? Once levels of fault are determined, the insurance adjustor will use a formulaic approach to calculating damages. Most carriers use formulas to calculate medical expenses and economic damages like loss of income or loss of property. In addition, the adjuster may modify the base number to reflect intangibles such as pain and suffering. Then fault will be apportioned to adjust this number.

This number will then provide a starting point for negotiations with the claimant for settlement purposes. If a settlement is reached, the insurance provider makes a payment to the claimant or the attorney and the matter is over. If no agreement is reached, however, litigation usually ensues and the court or arbitration panel becomes responsible for deciding the fortunes of both parties.

The Legal Team

The suitability of the legal team is essential to the success of litigation and ultimately the recovery of the investment. Defendants will constantly readjust their willingness to resolve claims based on their perception of how effective the plaintiff's counsel is at litigating a particular result. When lawyers are good, defendants feel pressure to resolve the claim before the table is set for a damaging verdict. However, when they believe they can out-lawyer (or outspend) the plaintiff, the disposition of a claim may take very long indeed.

The legal team also plays an indispensable role during the entire investment process. As investors evaluate an opportunity, the legal team provides information about the strengths and weaknesses of a claim. After the investment is made, they provide funders with periodic updates about the progress of the case. They should be thoroughly familiar with legal and procedural developments and timely disclose any material issues that may affect its outcome. If they are replaced as counsel, funders will need to know what happened and how any attorney substitution will affect their investment.

The legal team will usually serve as an escrow agent in the event of settlement, taking custody of any proceeds from the settlement and distributing those funds to investors, optimally before any payment is made to the client. If the case is lost, they are expected to provide funders with as much information as necessary regarding the circumstances of the loss to help them adjust their underwriting policies for future investments.

Most importantly, attorneys and their staff are responsible for guiding their clients though a long and complicated legal process. Lawyers and paralegals must clearly understand the issues of the case, as well the rules of evidence and civil procedure. They must be experts in handling the types of claims and clients being considered for investment. They should have adequate motivation and resources to bring the case to a successful conclusion.

A good legal team should include enough people to do the job right. For some smaller tort and commercial cases, a solo practitioner may be able to handle the entire matter. In more complex cases, a much larger team may be required, consisting of multiple lawyers, paralegals and administrative staff.

In many cases, it may not be possible to critically evaluate all of the above factors without being exposed to the same team for multiple investments. It is more likely that the legal team will be complete strangers to investors. For this reason, underwriters try to make reasonable assumptions about the legal team based on their backgrounds. These assumptions center on the attorneys' professional history. Basic elements like bar admissions will determine whether attorneys will be able to litigate in a particular jurisdiction or before a particular court. Where they studied law, where they have worked—and for how long—as well as how long they have been practicing in total are all valid considerations.

Any problems embedded in an attorney's background—disciplinary actions, sanctions, suspensions, or disbarments from any jurisdictions—should serve as glaring red flags. An attorney's practice history can also speak to their areas of expertise and lawyering style: have they handled similar cases in the past? Have they published articles in the relevant area of law? Is there information on them in the *Martindale-Hubbell Law Directory*?

Are there published court decisions available in which they served as counsel? How well drafted are their court documents? How strongly do they relate with clients—and in particular, how are their interactions with the client in the action in question? The answers to these questions allow underwriters to predict how successful an attorney is likely to be.

Similar background inquiries also speak volumes about a law firm. How complex is the case? Is the firm experienced with these types of claims? Do they possess adequate resources? Which firm members will do the work? What is their level of experience? Are other specialists available to help? What is their track record in similar claims? Does the firm have a strong reputation in their jurisdiction? How did they come to represent the plaintiff? Has the law firm worked with funding companies in the past?

Law firms must also possess adequate capital. Many funders make the mistake of assuming that litigation costs will not impact their investments when cases are on contingency simply because a law firm pays all of the costs. While this can be true with smaller consumer funding, cases with potentially high damages like catastrophic tort, medical malpractice, and business disputes require a much larger war chest than the typical tort case. What many fail to appreciate is that law firms are frequently thinly capitalized, a factor that impressive websites and knowledgeable attorneys can obscure. An unfortunate number of attorneys are prone to biting off more than they can chew, taking on cases they hope will result in quick settlements. When these quick settlements do not materialize, which is usually the case, they may pass on their cases to better-financed counsel, who may not be familiar with the terms of the legal finance investment. Alternatively, attorneys might drag their feet, sometimes for years, or even abandon cases entirely for lack of funding. More frequently, they will attempt to settle them for a much lower amount than the merits warrant, often for an amount insufficient to repay the funding company.

Underwriters must therefore possess a sound understanding of the costs involved in each claim being considered for funding and to evaluate the law firms' capacity to cover these costs. This is particularly important in high-stakes cases, both tort and commercial. It would be a concern, for example, if a small firm specializing in auto accidents suddenly embarked on representing a client in a products liability claim against a large manufacturer. Besides the obvious issues of know-how and experience, underwriters must understand how the law firm plans to finance this undertaking.

Damages

The amount of the alleged damages is an important indicator of a claim's size. However, the reasonableness of those estimates compared to the merits of the case and the defendant's ability to pay them is an even more critical consideration. The identification, measurement, and proof of damages are some of the most challenging aspects of civil litigation.

There are different types of damages that plaintiffs seek to recover. Compensatory damages cover actual injury or economic loss and are intended to restore the injured party to a pre-injury position. In some types of cases, such as contract disputes, there may also be consequential damages, which may include loss of profit or revenue, and may be recovered if it is determined such damages were reasonably foreseeable by the defendant. Punitive or exemplary damages are sometimes awarded above any other damages to punish a defendant for acts of gross negligence or intentional misconduct. Punitive damages are not awarded to compensate the plaintiff, but to deter the defendant and others in similar situations from repeating the same undesirable conduct. Conduct often associated with punitive damages includes bad faith, fraud, oppression, outrageous and violent acts, as well as situations where defendants acted intentionally, maliciously, or with utter disregard for the plaintiff's rights. Statutory damages are sometimes required by law. For example, in copyright infringement cases, plaintiffs may be entitled to certain minimum damages pursuant to federal statutes.

From the underwriter's perspective, the principal consideration of any damage estimate is reasonableness. The calculation of damages is an area where the legal team's creativity can make a significant impact. Plaintiffs may provide expert testimony demonstrating a catastrophic damage model, while defendants will attack the credibility of the plaintiff's experts and perhaps even offer their own contradictory version of damages. In many cases, damage estimates produced by plaintiffs' counsel are very ambitious, whereas those offered by defendants are unreasonably low. As with many things, the truth is somewhere in the middle, and the underwriter must strip away the window dressing and subterfuge to gain a realistic understanding about the potential size of an award or settlement.

It is generally difficult to predict award or settlement outcomes with any degree of specificity. The parties attempt to prove their view of damages through objective evidence and expert testimony, which are typically produced by the plaintiffs' legal team only during the late stages of litigation, frequently leaving underwriters on their own to determine damages during the earlier stages of the claim. Underwriters must consider all the circumstances of the claim to arrive at a high/low range for any potential award or settlement. While imprecise at times, this analysis helps them predict whether a potential recovery will be sufficient to compensate all of the stakeholders.

Some of the most precarious damage estimates relate to injuries or losses that are too remote, uncertain, or contingent. Estimates must be predicated upon sufficient evidence that justifies a damage award. A plaintiff cannot be compensated for a speculative probability of future loss unless he or she can prove that such consequences can reasonably be expected to occur. Consequential damages are often difficult to validate as a result. In commercial claims, for example, plaintiffs frequently encounter problems when seeking to recover lost profits for new businesses, usually on the grounds that such profits are unduly speculative. For this reason, underwriters typically consider only those damages that are directly supported by objective evidence and are apparent without complex analysis or justification. They will disregard most consequential, punitive, and often even statutory damages to arrive at a conservative baseline model for their funding decision.

Liens and Other Encumbrances

Liens are claims of third parties on a portion of the future proceeds recovered by plaintiffs from defendants. Individual tort and commercial cases can be subject to numerous liens from attorneys, medical providers, other legal finance companies, government entities, and private individuals. In addition, portfolios of cases can also be subject to liens, primarily from financial institutions and investors. The presence of too many liens, whether known or unknown, can potentially increase the number of stakeholders, thereby diluting everyone's ownership interest. From a funder's perspective, excessive liens are undesirable because they decrease the amount of proceeds available for distribution and cloud the priority of payments for all involved.

In consumer transactions, almost all lawsuits involving personal injury have liens from third parties. The primary lien is for attorney's fees, which is typically a third of any recovery, but in some circumstances can be as high as 50 percent of the recovery.[4] This lien always comes first, regardless of any other liens created before or after an investor becomes involved. Other liens include medical providers, Medicaid, workers compensation, Social Security and disability, child support, IRS or state tax authorities, and other funding companies, among others.

In commercial deals, it is also common to see third-party liens. If the attorney is on contingency, there will be a lien from the attorney. There may be civil judgments, as well as liens from the IRS, state, and sometimes foreign tax authorities, expert witnesses and other legal services providers, as well as legal finance companies and occasionally individuals who invested in the claim.

Lien analysis is a vital consideration for any underwriter because even if the merits, procedural posture, and other elements of a case are compelling enough to suggest a win, an investor still risks nonpayment if other stakeholders are entitled to a priority distribution from those proceeds.

Ultimately, lien law governs the distribution of legal finance proceeds. Perfected liens[5] usually trump all unperfected liens, meaning that "first in time, first in right" does not always apply. However, even this perfected lien rule has several exceptions. For instance, federal liens (a notable example being Medicare liens) take priority over almost anything. Many attorneys will not even release funds until they have received a clearance letter from Medicare.[6]

State liens are also a concern for providers. One of the most common state liens is for child support, where the plaintiff owes their local social services agency money for the support of one or more children. As a general rule, child support liens will trump legal finance liens, even where one can show the legal finance lien occurred and was perfected before the support lien. As a matter of public policy, the legal finance lien will be subject to the child's interests.

Unfortunately, novice investors often ignore lien analysis to their detriment, only to find several years later that their investments are worth significantly less than expected. An understanding of lien law and a thorough lien search are both essential to a well-conceived underwriting methodology. Underwriters must inquire with plaintiffs and their legal teams, and conduct independent research to obtain an accurate record of present and possible future encumbrances to the recovery proceeds. Many of the liens can be discovered by performing a background check on all the plaintiffs (individual or corporate) that will be parties to the investment agreement, using Bloomberg Law, Intelius, LexisNexis, and Westlaw. In larger deals, funding companies may require plaintiffs to furnish their credit reports to discover any liens, judgments, bankruptcies, or potential future claims.

Bankruptcy

Bankruptcy is a legal process to restructure debt by insolvent individuals and entities, which may affect the payment rights for all investors relying on the bankrupt counterparty's promises to pay. In many financial transactions where the settlement date is in the future, the prospect of a bankruptcy proceeding affecting the payor's obligation is an important consideration for funders. This is a very real risk in legal finance transactions because many plaintiffs are financially distressed and may be teetering near bankruptcy. The bankruptcy proceeding will usually try to include the plaintiff's future lawsuit recovery in the bankruptcy trust for payment to third parties, despite any language in the funding agreement excluding the proceeds of a settlement from the bankruptcy trust.

Currently, the treatment of legal finance proceeds in bankruptcy proceedings is inconsistent across various jurisdictions, and the results of any future actions are generally unpredictable. There is a real risk that lawsuit investors may be last in line to collect. It is critical, therefore, to identify whether the applicant is undergoing bankruptcy or likely to file for bankruptcy while the claim is pending.

Structuring

Once the underwriting phase is completed, funding companies will structure a transaction with the plaintiff and the attorney. In consumer deals, the structure is usually identical for most investments, insofar as most cases have similar requirements. In some situations, funders are required to adapt their investment agreements to accommodate multiple investments, buyouts of previous funding liens, or other atypical funding arrangements. In commercial claims, however, there is far greater diversity from case to case, generally because the plaintiffs' circumstances require a bespoke product or because the lawsuits themselves are inherently more complex.

The investment agreement is the primary mechanism for controlling after-the-fact risk in legal finance transactions. It sets forth the rights and obligations of investors, plaintiffs, and their attorneys. It will restrict certain types of activities which are detrimental to investors, while requiring timely disclosure and cooperation from all parties involved. In drafting effective investment agreements, a balance must exist between creating well-reasoned, airtight documents and the practicalities of marketing financial products to clients and attorneys. After all, agreements that are too complicated and onerous may inadvertently discourage prospective clients or their attorneys from doing the funder's deals. This holds particular importance in the highly competitive context of tort advances, where transactions occur with much greater frequency.

My experience with drafting investment agreements in this space involved a constant effort to strike this balance. As one of the first legal finance companies, we did not have the benefit of relying on shared industry experience to guide our first investments as companies do today. As a result, our funding agreements for tort advances, attorney funding, and commercial deals were essentially products of trial and error.

The initial agreements were very basic, including only key terms of the deal and often omitting restrictions or penalty provisions. Those agreements naively idealized legal finance as a gentlemen's club, where clients' and attorneys' behavior would be tempered by notions of fair play, courtesy and professional responsibility. The reality, however, was starkly different. There were—and still are—clients and attorneys who defaulted on their agreements for a variety of reasons. Some brokers referred cases but acted unscrupulously. Competing funding companies advanced money to the same client, sometimes simultaneously. Some attorneys obscured liens from underwriters and then lied about the status of our investments. Other attorneys withdrew from representation without informing us or simply refused to cooperate for no particular reason. We encountered client fraud, attorney fraud, and everything in between.

As a result of the lessons we learned, each successive generation of our agreements attempted to close vulnerabilities that were exposed every time another deal did not go as planned. Over the years, our initial three-page tort agreement eventually grew to 15 pages and our seven-page commercial agreement reached 55 pages. At the same time, however, our ability to close deals suffered as clients and attorneys alike balked at signing our complex contracts, especially in light of increased competition from new companies that had not yet learned these lessons. We finally accepted that some risks can never be drafted away, and that trying too hard to do so only antagonized our client base. As a result, our current agreements are streamlined to provide maximum protection without being overly technical, obtrusive, or onerous for either our clients or their attorneys.

Investment agreements must also be versatile. Because lawsuit funders generally operate across many different markets, it is important that agreements are consistent with laws and requirements in all jurisdictions where business is conducted. For example, the assignment of proceeds is a sale and purchase transaction that enables most deals in the tort advance niche. As discussed in Chapter 6 in greater detail, some states do not allow the assignment of proceeds recovered from personal injury claims. Agreements in jurisdictions that prohibit assignments, therefore, should always include the appropriate alternative legal theories on which investment transactions rely (e.g., promise to pay). Funding contracts should also be easy to understand for all consumers and consistent with the relevant state's plain English laws.

Over the years, the American Legal Finance Association has encouraged best practices for funding agreements to ensure transparency and fair dealing in consumer transactions. For example, ALFA members now use agreements that meet the requirements of the New York attorney general for legal finance contracts with New York consumers, and many members use similar agreements with consumers in other states as well.

Pricing and Payment

Economic considerations form the foundation of a lawsuit investment. All the parties involved should maintain realistic expectations regarding the investor's return. The agreement's pricing structure should compensate the investor for the changing profile of claim's risk as the lawsuit evolves. As expected, investors often have unique perspectives about risk and return, divergent risk tolerance, and differing abilities to evaluate that risk. This renders legal finance products pricing a very individualized process.

A good starting point is considering the risk involved in the case. Assessing what return one can expect for a given amount of risk helps to determine a base number. Capital costs are another important consideration. Origination, underwriting and servicing expenses may also contribute to the financing rate. What are the origination costs? Did the case cost more to originate than others? Did a broker refer the case? Who pays the broker's commission? How much did underwriting cost in this case? Did it exceed the cost in other cases? Did meeting the plaintiffs or their counsel incur travel expenses? What is the cost of servicing these investments? How long will the resolution likely take? What if the parties reach a settlement earlier than expected: will there be a sufficient return for taking the risk? What if the case drags on for years? What if it goes to trial? What if it is appealed? Will follow-on investments be needed? What if budgets are overrun? What will it cost if litigation is needed to collect?

Budgeting and Aligning Payment Arrangements in Commercial Deals

In commercial matters where the litigation expenses are being financed by a legal finance provider, the added risk of cost overruns must be addressed prior to consummating the investment. A funder's commitment to invest in a claim cannot be open-ended, as it would be very difficult to evaluate the risk and economics of such a transaction. Investors need a clear understanding of how much their share of the expenses will be and what is required to finish the lawsuit.

In a typical scenario, the funder pledges an investment amount to pay for a portion or all of the projected expenses, which is paid all at once or in a series of investments, perhaps a portion every month, by quarter, dependent on certain litigation milestones, or as they come due. What would happen if these expenses were much higher than originally projected? At this point, the funder must decide whether to continue funding the case. It may ask to renegotiate the terms of the investment agreement or decide to discontinue funding the case altogether if the investment agreement permits it. When paying the costs of litigation, investors must properly structure the relationship with attorneys to take into account the potential for cost overruns.

While this advice may seem banal, a surprising number of legal finance providers repeat this mistake over and over again. When it comes to lawyers, cost overruns are the norm rather than the exception. The entire premise of law firms' current pay model is to bill as much as possible for as long as possible. Hourly lawyers have little incentive or training to plan ahead when it comes to expenses and budgets. They are often inept at it and they dislike doing it. Instead, they simply react to whatever their opponent does and then bill their clients accordingly. By contrast, a lawsuit investor cannot make open-ended commitments any more than a developer considering a real estate project can.

When paying litigation expenses, the investment process should include setting a comprehensive and realistic budget for the case. This will also help the provider determine whether to fund the claim in the first place. The budgeting process is not a simple exercise, as lawsuits have many moving parts to consider, but if every claim is reduced to its component parts, budgeting becomes a lot easier. For example, each claim has common stages like investigating the matter, conducting legal research, engaging in discovery, trial preparation, and so on. How much would it cost to draft the pleadings? How much for depositions? Which experts are needed and how much do they cost? How does this opponent litigate its cases? Is this a comparatively fast or slow jurisdiction? How efficient is the judge in this case? Using this methodology, a corresponding cost is assigned to each activity and each sub-task. The sum of all the tasks will comprise the litigation budget.

In evaluating the budget, investors must also discern the reasonableness of any projected expense. To facilitate this, funders can compile a database for different expenses, either from past cases funded by the investor or any other cases where the budgets and final costs are available, and apply them as benchmarks for future budgets.

Once the budget is estimated, the funder must ensure that the funding commitment is aligned with the attorneys' commitment to litigate the case. There are several strategies for attaining this alignment. One of the most effective approaches is to have the attorneys agree on a flat fee for their representation. When attorneys agree to a flat fee, the budget can be properly allocated among different service providers, without the risk that excessive attorney billings will eat into funds previously apportioned to other expense items, like expert witnesses, for example. Similarly, attorneys can agree to cap their fees at a certain amount or a percentage of the budget. In some cases, funders have required attorneys to provide further discounts if their estimates regarding litigation expenses turned out to be unreasonably low. Whatever the arrangement, it is critical for lawsuit investors to properly structure their investment to prevent cost overruns from negatively affecting their ability to finance the claim and reducing their ultimate return.

Payments Management

As previously noted, another potential problem for funders of commercial cases occurs when plaintiffs use investment proceeds for purposes other than paying for the agreed to litigation costs. For example, suppose a funder provides $500,000 to the plaintiff to pay for expert witnesses that will testify regarding the reasonableness of his damage model. Instead of spending the money on experts, however, the plaintiff uses the proceeds for working capital to keep his business solvent. While this example is extreme —as it would deal a mortal blow to the underlying lawsuit—it nevertheless demonstrates how perilous the misuse of investment funds can be. It is essential, therefore, to ensure that investment proceeds earmarked toward particular purposes are deployed as intended.

To mitigate this risk, funders typically require the proceeds of their investment to be transferred to an escrow agent, usually a lawyer nominated by the investor, who will determine the reasonableness of any invoice and pay the expenses as necessary directly to service providers. For example, in a $500,000 funding transaction where $100,000 will go to operating expenses, $100,000 to personal expenses of the plaintiff, and $300,000 to experts, the funder will pay the first $100,000 directly to the plaintiff and deposit the balance with an escrow agent for deployment in accordance with the terms of the investment agreement—the escrow agent will pay the company and the experts directly.

Governing Law, Forum, and Venue

Funders should have a rational expectation as to how their funding agreements will be treated by courts and regulators in the event a dispute arises after an investment is made. As in any business, situations often arise where counterparties will not or cannot fulfill their contractual obligations and litigation to enforce those rights occurs. As of this writing, the legal and regulatory environment relating to this industry remains quite fluid (see Chapter 6). Several states have introduced legislation dealing with legal finance transactions, while a few have discouraged activity in this space or even outlawed it via adverse case law, regulatory action, or both. Some courts have been very outspoken about their views on legal finance and a number have taken activist positions against the industry.

Moreover, most legal finance providers invest across multiple jurisdictions and some invest internationally.[7] In this context, funders often find themselves defending their contracts in unfamiliar territory, as they must simultaneously contend with multiple disputes and collection efforts against parties from different jurisdictions. Providers strive to keep the costs of these disputes to a minimum, but litigating in a distant or unfamiliar forum is expensive and risky.

One valuable method of minimizing these risks is to ensure that investors can bring a lawsuit or defend themselves as close to home as possible. Funders and their attorneys prefer to appear in a local courthouse, in front of judges with whom they are familiar, before juries whose disposition and values they understand, and subject to law and rules of procedure with which they are well acquainted. Gaining the home field advantage, therefore, is an important strategic consideration for litigants. Funders should stipulate in advance in their funding agreements which governing law will be used and where the dispute will be heard. Courts will generally enforce these provisions so long as they are fair and reasonable.

This presumes, however, that the investor's "home" is suitable for legal finance to begin with, which may not always be the case. Investors must be careful that their default jurisdictions provide outcomes that are reasonably predictable. The home field advantage is only valuable if it actually offers the benefits sought, rather than the illusion of advantage.

Issues relating to governing law, venue, and forum as reflected in the investment agreement are perhaps the most important considerations for mitigating after-the-fact risk. For this reason, it is important to consider to what extent those factors are favorable to the investor's business and how long they will continue to be so. Does the investor do a lot of business in these markets? Is there a licensing requirement to operate there? In the event of a dispute, which jurisdiction's (state, country, etc.) laws apply? And in which forum: state court, federal court or arbitration? The analysis of these issues should consider past legal precedent in the jurisdictions being considered. How do state and federal courts treat legal finance contracts in that state? For example, how do they view champerty, maintenance, and barratry? How about usury? What about assignment? What was the result of past litigation in this area? Do other lawsuit investors use these jurisdictions as their governing law? Are any bills pending in their legislatures that may alter the status quo?

Many tort investors use New York as their default jurisdiction, while many commercial investors use Texas. New York and Texas have traditionally been viewed as safe states by lawsuit investors due to their sophisticated court systems and pro-business climates. However, New York still has champerty statutes and some anomalous case precedent adverse to legal finance. It also has a bill pending to regulate consumer legal finance transactions. Similarly, in Texas a legislative committee has recently studied the impact and desirability of legal finance in that state. This is not to imply that New York and Texas are no longer viable jurisdictions for legal finance. In fact, both states have had recent positive developments that have raised their profile as default jurisdictions for lawsuit investors. Instead, the example demonstrates that these issues are often nuanced, requiring a great deal of research and deliberation.

In some cases, it may make sense to bypass U.S. law entirely. For example, Burford, like its competitor Juridica, was originally organized in the United Kingdom and has an international infrastructure to support its investment activities. Burford uses special offshore vehicles to fund certain transactions and uses English law as its governing law in those deals. This can be a very effective strategy. Since English law is more developed compared to unsettled U.S. state laws relating to legal finance, this can be a prudent risk control mechanism, as foreign judgments are readily enforceable in the United States.

It is also possible to bypass courts by designating arbitration as the forum. A majority of providers require binding arbitration in their finance agreements as the default forum for any dispute. Arbitration is often used for the resolution of commercial disputes, and is particularly useful in the legal funding context. As discussed, arbitration is a private forum for alternative dispute resolution. In arbitration, an independent arbitrator or panel of arbitrators reviews the case and imposes a decision that is legally binding on both sides. It offers a number of advantages over judicial proceedings:

- When the subject matter of the dispute is highly technical, arbitrators with an appropriate degree of expertise can be appointed (as one cannot "choose the judge" in litigation).

- Arbitration is often faster, cheaper and more flexible for businesses than litigation in court.

- Most arbitration rules do not require that parties be represented by an attorney.

- Arbitration proceedings and an arbitral award are generally confidential, rather than public as with court decisions.

While funders will always enjoy a psychological advantage in their "home" jurisdiction, prudent investors should also ensure that the law in their default jurisdiction is actually favorable toward legal finance transactions. Bypassing U.S. law is an option for investors with international infrastructures. The designation of arbitration as the forum of dispute resolution is another option for sidestepping courts altogether.

Order of Payments

Frequently, multiple parties may be entitled to a portion of the lawsuit's proceeds. In a typical transaction this includes the lawyer, the funding company, and the claimant—usually in that order. However, quite often other parties may be involved. This can occur where a deal is being funded by co-investors or where the attorneys are not retained on a contingency basis.

The order of payments sets forth the waterfall for any payments that are made to the parties after receiving compensation from the defendants. This is especially important when the recovery is too small to pay everyone. Who is to be paid first? Is the attorney compensated before the funder and the client? How is the attorney, investor, or client compensated for litigation costs? How do multiple investors share the proceeds among themselves? Whatever the reason, the order of payments for recoveries is an important consideration for investors and should reflect the well-informed understanding of all parties.

Multiple Claimants and Inter-Claimant Agreement

Funders sometimes invest in claims that involve two or more related or affiliated plaintiffs. This may be because two claimants may have substantially similar claims against the same or related defendants. In the tort context, for example, this may occur when relatives have a joint claim for the wrongful death of a family member. In a commercial setting, this could occur when similarly situated shareholders are squeezed out of a company and then sue for compensation.

Defendants frequently view their liability in terms of events rather than to the individuals or companies suing them. As a result, they may allocate a specific amount to resolve the liability that flows from that event. The specific outcome for each similarly situated claimant, therefore, is not the primary consideration. This is true in lawsuits involving toxic spills, airline crashes, and even securities fraud. For this reason, defendants may be willing to tolerate, and perhaps even encourage, very different results for plaintiffs, despite a common fact pattern that led to the dispute.

As a result, two or more nearly identical lawsuits can produce very different results, even for related parties. Where the plaintiffs are mother and daughter, for example, this may not matter very much. If they are close relatives, they may have an expectation that any proceeds will be divided in some informal but equitable way. However, when the claimants are not so related, there is potential for confusion, bickering, and ultimately further litigation to settle these rights.

An example that comes readily to mind involves two plaintiffs who have nearly identical claims, agree to pool their resources, share information, and perhaps even hire the same attorney. What happens, for argument sake, if the defendant offers $1 million to resolve both claims? How will the two claimants share that $1 million settlement? How will this affect the investor?

This situation creates two problems for the funder. The first is the problem of confusion. The claimants may have their unique perspectives regarding the outcome of the claim. Each may feel he or she contributed more to the settlement and should be entitled to a greater share of the proceeds. In the absence of specific guidelines in the funding agreement on how to deal with this situation, infighting among claimants can complicate the return calculation, while holding up payment.

The second is the problem of circumvention. Again, depending on how the agreement is structured, lopsided settlements can exploit weaknesses in the funding agreement. In the mother and daughter example, the settlement can be arranged in such a way that most, if not all, of the proceeds are funneled to the family member that is not party to the agreement.

It is critical, therefore, to draft transaction documents to limit exposure to these scenarios. This can be achieved by binding all of the potential plaintiffs with the investment contract and clearly defining what will happen if the resolution of the claim yields disparate settlement amounts. In some cases, it may help to include an inter-claimant agreement—where the plaintiffs agree among themselves to the exact division of proceeds as part of the deal documents. In such an arrangement, two similarly situated plaintiffs may commit to evenly divide any recovery or may define a different formula for sharing the proceeds.

Any obligations on the part of the claimants should be joint and severable. Both parties must adhere to the requirements of the transaction documents or face liability if the other breaches any of the obligations. Mutual liability is an effective tool for mitigating events of default.

Non-Recourse Investment

The majority of lawsuit investments are non-recourse. This means that, subject to certain exceptions, the lawsuit investor is entitled only to a share of the proceeds recovered from the underlying claim and not any other assets of the plaintiff. There are no personal guarantees, for instance. Since lawsuits are speculative and most investments in this space occur prior to the adjudication of the claim, the plaintiffs' obligation to pay investors is triggered only upon the successful recovery of moneys from one or several defendants.

This is a critical feature of most legal finance products (loans to law firms being a notable exception). It distinguishes them from loans, the repayment of which is absolute rather than contingent.

Loan transactions may be subject to various restrictions imposed by state usury laws applicable to individuals and businesses.

Not all legal finance transactions are structured as non-recourse transactions. Some commercial deals, especially patent and bankruptcy investments, may involve an acquisition of an asset which is the subject or plaintiff in litigation. By acquiring the rights to a patent, one may sue anyone infringing that patent. Similarly, by buying a book of receivables in bankruptcy one may sue to collect on them. Also, many loans to law firms are structured as ordinary loans secured by the firm's portfolio of legal receivables.

As a general matter, usury rates cap returns at a level far below even the most optimistic break-even assumptions in lawsuit funding, creating a significant disincentive to invest funds at the same rate as more secure loans. Business loans, however, are frequently exempted from usury caps in many states when the size of the loan is above a certain threshold. The risk of usury, therefore, is a more important consideration in smaller deals with individual consumers.

To avoid any confusion with a loan, if the investment is non-recourse, funders will include language clearly stating this in the funding agreement. U.S. courts have generally accepted this distinction between lawsuit investments and conventional loans. For a financing transaction to be usurious, it must have the most important feature of a loan: it must create an absolute obligation on the part of the recipient to repay it without regard to any circumstances that may excuse such repayment. If an obligation is contingently repayable and not absolutely, there can be no usury, though courts have generally required that the risk of such a contingency—namely losing the case—must be substantial and not too remote.

Common Attorney Undertakings

Attorneys and law firms have a great deal of impact on the outcome of claims and investor returns. At the outset, funders have a set of expectations about the lawsuit and their ability to collect on the investment which is based to a large extent on the attorney's representations regarding the case. Interaction with attorneys is critical to assessing issues like the merits of the case, the existence of third-party liens, the firm's capacity to fund the claim, the availability of appropriate expert witnesses, the firm's willingness to provide disclosure to the investor during the pendency of the claim, and their commitment to pay the investor in accordance with the funding agreement if there is a recovery. In many cases, the attorney will take custody of any settlement proceeds after the claim is resolved and will determine when and how much to pay all of the stakeholders. How does one make sure the attorney does what he or she promised?

A key feature of most investment agreements is the attorney's undertaking or acknowledgement, which is a series of covenants requiring the attorney to cooperate with the terms of the investments agreement between the funder and plaintiff, and obligating the attorney to engage in or refrain from certain actions. They include, among other things, the obligation to: (1) disclose all assignments, transfers and liens on the proceeds of the claim; (2) keep the investor updated about the progress of the case; (3) provide written notice of withdrawal and contact details for new counsel if there is an attorney substitution; (4) distribute the proceeds to the investors according to the agreement; and (5) keep the investor's share of the proceeds in a separate trust account in the event of a dispute. In some situations, funders will also require negative covenants that compel the attorney, for example, to refrain from signing any subsequent undertakings with other funders that may dilute or encumber the payment to the original investor. These covenants can be further expanded to include additional obligations if the nature of the deal requires further assurances.

An attorney's undertaking provides a clear explanation of the attorney's role vis-à-vis the investor and is an integral part of the investment agreement, particularly in consumer tort deals and commercial transactions where the law firm also acts as the custodian of the investor's portion of the proceeds. While there are no guarantees that attorneys will abide by these covenants, they do nevertheless provide a basis for investors to insist on certain conduct on the part of the attorney, and may also create liability for the attorney if they are breached.

Plaintiffs' Obligation to Cooperate

The plaintiffs' duty to cooperate with their legal team undergirds the investment decision. At the time of the investment, the prospect of recovery is completely speculative, since no legally exercisable right yet exists to compel the defendant to make payment. The entire claim rests on the plaintiff's desire and determination to enforce his or her rights. If clients do not cooperate with their attorneys or decide to abandon their underlying claims, investments in those cases will likely be compromised.

In many personal injury cases, like automobile accidents for example, the legal team can access much of the objective evidence without the plaintiffs' involvement. Attorneys can obtain documents like police reports, ambulance records and property damage estimates directly from the source of information. The plaintiffs' cooperation in a personal injury case mostly relates to receiving medical treatment, which is usually a priority for plaintiffs after an accident anyway.

Investors are particularly sensitive about plaintiff cooperation when funding complex matters, especially business disputes, malpractice actions, product liability suits, intellectual property claims and other cases that are based on contract law, statutory law or tort. Plaintiffs play a major role in developing these types of cases. They may need to educate their legal team about their industry, as well as the facts and circumstances that led to the dispute. They are frequently responsible for furnishing counsel with relevant documentary evidence necessary to prove their cases and make themselves available to testify at depositions and in court. They are instrumental in recommending appropriate witnesses who should be called to testify and can also help their attorneys neutralize the testimony of defense witnesses. Plaintiffs will typically spend many hours with the legal team answering questions, refining strategy, and preparing testimony. Without their cooperation and active engagement cases cannot proceed.

Plaintiffs' circumstances can change, however. They can move to different states or countries. They may resolve their differences with defendants outside the legal system without the attorney's knowledge. When plaintiffs are companies, their management and business models can change, sometimes leading to changes in their risk appetites and litigation capabilities. Companies might embark on new business opportunities and lose interest in pending litigation. They could secure new financing or merge with other businesses, which reduces their need for a lawsuit victory. Who, then, should bear this risk?

Investors should accept that they have little to no control over plaintiffs' whims. For this reason, when vetting investment prospects it is also critical to consider how the plaintiffs' level of engagement may change over time. It may be necessary to evaluate their business prospects or any material events that may affect their capacity, motivation and commitment to engage in protracted litigation. For most funders, the obligation that litigants will use their best efforts to prosecute claims is irrevocable. Any contravention of their duty to cooperate will generally trigger a default under the funding agreement, exposing the client to direct liability. If circumstances change causing plaintiffs to lose interest in their cases or if they are uncooperative with the process for other reasons, funders will seek to recover from them any investments made up to that point. It is therefore essential to include appropriate language in the investment agreement clearly stipulating what will happen should the plaintiff fail to cooperate on a best efforts basis.

Authority to Control or Settle Claim

As previously discussed, plaintiffs and their legal teams—and not lawsuit investors—are presumed to control litigation in the United States. Even as this view continues to evolve, American courts are not generally tolerant of any interference with the attorney-client relationship. Courts fully expect plaintiffs and their attorneys to make the final decisions on retaining (or firing) lawyers, approving legal strategies, and accepting settlements. For this reason, many investors specifically state in their funding agreements that there is no transfer of the underlying cause of action. In addition, many also specify that they do not have any right to direct or influence the litigation in any way. Many agreements also make clear that only the plaintiffs themselves have the right to approve settlements.

As mentioned, this approach has some notable exceptions. For instance, in patent and bankruptcy deals where the underlying asset is partially or wholly acquired prior to litigation, investors can exercise full control over the litigation process and the settlement of claims. Outside of the usual exceptions, great care should be taken in drafting agreements to avoid any inference that funders, rather than clients and their attorneys, are directing or controlling litigation.

Compliance

The consummation of the funding transaction does not end the legal finance investment process. Funders must be vigilant and proactive in managing their investments throughout the entire life cycle of the claim. Every case has unique circumstances that will affect how it develops and ultimately resolves. Critical events may unexpectedly occur that completely change the dynamics of investments. Cases may be lost or dismissed. Others may yield recoveries too small to pay all the stakeholders. Many factors can potentially deprive investors of their return, so they must be ready to intervene at any moment to preserve the benefit of their bargain. A striking number of investors, however, pay little attention to post-investment policies like follow-up and collections, which are an essential part of properly managing these types of assets.

An effective compliance strategy is not only needed to deal with emerging problems related to each investment. It is a proactive approach, responsible for overseeing every stage of the investment process by staying ahead of material events while also using appropriate measures to mitigate problems and predict what could be avoided. It involves data management, case status management, payments management, investigations, dispute resolution, and collections.

While the investment agreement sets forth the funders' rights and remedies, a detailed compliance policy is also necessary when rights must be exercised. What specific action will a funder's team take if something threatens their investment? How will they respond to discount requests? What will happen if there is not enough money to pay all stakeholders? What will they do if the attorney does not return their calls after they invest? What steps will they take if the client instructs their attorney not to pay them? What happens when an attorney withdraws from a case? What if there is an attempt by the parties to circumvent the funding agreement?

After investment, funders keep track of their deals by periodically contacting attorneys regarding the progress of those claims. This typically occurs once every several months for the average case and more frequently for larger investments. In commercial claims, where the stakes are higher, update requests occur even more frequently. Some providers have weekly, biweekly or monthly conversations with the legal team and the plaintiff regarding the development of the case.

In addition to contacting law firms for updates, funding companies may also check publicly available court records to verify the procedural status of cases, especially if they encounter any abnormalities. Court records are often available online. Most states have websites where providers can access them, usually using the docket number, the case caption, and sometimes the attorney's name. State court records can also be examined in person. Procedural histories can often be checked by calling the appropriate court and speaking with a records clerk. Federal court documents and procedural histories are available online through Pacer.

At some point, a funder may discover that a case is close to resolution or that the attorney has already received payment from the defendant. It then notifies the parties how much is due under the investment agreement by invoicing the client and attorney.

Payment

There are many situations in the market today where attorneys have settled on a preferred provider, and some relationships have spanned many years. Other attorneys use several different providers whom they trust to provide services to their clients. After a case is resolved, the attorney usually receives the defendant's payment, deposits proceeds into an escrow account, and then pays himself, the funding company, any lien holders, and finally the client.

However, a large number of transactions in the market occur between attorneys and funders who are strangers to one another. This fledgling cooperation can often be tense. Such tension is a confluence of many factors. Breakdowns in communication between the parties are common. Many cases experience compliance issues because attorneys become reluctant to communicate information about their cases when they are not progressing as originally represented to investors. Funders need to determine how their cases are developing, how they should value them, and how their rights may be affected so they can make informed decisions about managing their investments. But attorneys may be embarrassed about recommending a bad investment or concerned with their own liability.

Other factors also contribute to this tension.

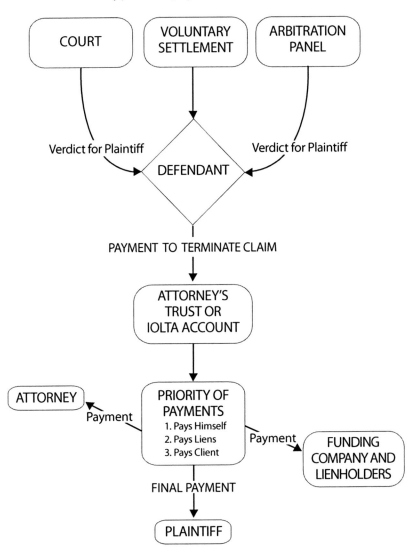

Typical Repayment Process

For instance, many cases experience unexpected events which require the parties to alter some part of their initial bargain. In addition, plaintiffs may exert pressure on attorneys to reduce payments to lien holders. Moreover, the entire investment process is a complex relationship management project, where parties pursue a common interest, but not always the same agenda. The management of that process frequently leads to disputes about the division of proceeds that are recovered from defendants.

Imagine for a moment that a company invests in an employment discrimination lawsuit, but once the matter reaches resolution, there does not appear to be enough proceeds to satisfy every bill and lien. As the trial date approaches, the attorney discovers that his client withheld critical information about previous employers, significantly damaging her claim. To avoid the risk of losing at trial, they settle for just a fraction of their original demand. The plaintiff's attorney presents a long list of bills and liens, proposing that the funder accept whatever portion of the settlement he deems appropriate. His offer is much lower than they were expecting. How should the funder handle this scenario?

Discount Requests

Most post-investment problems relate to issues of payment, the most common being requests for discounts. Many of these requests come as a result of material events which negatively affect cases, requiring all stakeholders to adjust their expectations. A significant number, however, do not in fact stem from any adverse changes, but rather opportunistic attempts by plaintiffs and their attorneys to renegotiate the terms of the deal.

Discount requests usually occur before a case is resolved and tend to happen closer to the disposition of a matter. As the parties' options narrow, their expectations regarding the outcome of their claims often grow more sober. This could result from a defendant's offer to settle or a recommendation made by a judge, arbitrator, or mediator. It could stem from a clearer understanding of the plaintiff's own damages, perhaps as a result of an expert witness report used to establish the damages claim.

Whatever the catalyst, plaintiffs' and their attorneys' expectations about what they are willing to accept inevitably evolve. At the time of the investment, many plaintiffs' expectations are overly optimistic, without regard to the complexity of the process and the reality of much lower settlement prospects. When reality sets in, claimants often feel motivated to attempt to enlarge their share of the recovery at the expense of investors or even their attorney.

The most common reasons for a discount request are either a low settlement or too many liens. Some cases settle for a much lower amount than the parties originally expected, frequently where the low recovery is not enough to pay the investors their entire return, or sometimes even their principal.

In other situations, the existence of too many liens, whether known or unknown to the funder, can potentially increase the number of stakeholders, thereby diluting everyone's ownership interest. If the case was resolved, but the attorney cannot pay the full amount due to other liens (including investments from other legal finance providers), the funder will need to determine the priority of these liens.

In many cases, a unique set of circumstances may require the funder to accept less money than originally agreed to, but this decision must be made only after it understands all of the circumstances surrounding the request. There is no universal formula for determining the right discount. All providers have unique perspectives regarding their returns. Considerations like their cost of capital, origination and processing costs, as well as the possible collection costs if they do not agree to a certain outcome will inevitably drive their decision of what is an acceptable return. In some instances, making discount accommodations may not be supported by the circumstances of the case, and investors may prefer to hold their ground. In others, providing a discount is a pragmatic compromise that can facilitate an investor's attainment of a target return.

Determining Lien Priority

As mentioned, liens play an important role in legal finance deals. The effectiveness of a compliance department centers largely on its knowledge of lien law. When fighting for its proper share of assigned proceeds, the funders must review information received from the attorney thoroughly, sorting through the liens and making a distinction between statutory, perfected, and unperfected liens, and those not listed in the contract or those that have followed the non-recourse investment. The existence of a lien and its amount should be verified by examining third-party records.[8]

Whenever a question regarding lien priority or a challenge of liens arises, a useful tool can be found in the funding agreement itself. The time when a legal finance provider can make the greatest impact is often before the investment is actually made. Ensuring that the proper remedies are outlined in the agreement before a problem arises is crucial to strengthening the funder's side of the bargain at a later date. Requiring a plaintiff's attorney to list existing liens prior to the investment will preclude certain unforeseeable issues from surfacing once the case is resolved.[9]

Attorney Substitutions

The investor's comfort level with the specific attorney handling the case always exerts a strong influence on the investment decision. Perhaps the attorney has a good reputation, an excellent track record or seemed sincere in his description of the case. Maybe the underwriter trusted the attorney to be a custodian of settlement proceeds if the case settles. Yet what happens if the attorney who knows the circumstances of the deal withdraws from the case?

The reality is that attorneys often change, and when they do, lawsuit investors are usually the last to know. Most funders discover this when calling law firms to get an update. They ask to speak to an attorney about a case and are informed that the firm "no longer represents that client," or perhaps that "this attorney is no longer with our firm."

These words usually herald trouble. Since all the assumptions were based on information gleaned from the first attorney, who also signed the investment agreement, how will his departure affect the case? Whenever there is a break-up between clients and their attorneys, it is important to understand why it happened. Who was the initiator of the break-up? Did the outgoing attorney lose confidence in the claim? Was the client not happy with the representation? Did the case run out of money? Did the attorney leave the firm?

When attorneys withdraw from representation, it is incumbent upon investors to act quickly to protect their investments. Even if nothing material changed in the case, an investor should make several inquiries: is the new attorney qualified to take over? Is he aware of this deal? After all, if the new attorney doesn't know about the deal with the plaintiff, he doesn't know about the obligation to pay the investor if the case is resolved. And more importantly, will he cooperate with an agreement signed by his predecessor?

As a general rule, most attorneys are bound by the rules of their state bar associations governing the safekeeping of property belonging to third parties. Specifically, the majority of states have adopted the American Bar Association's Model Rule 1.15, which requires that a "lawyer shall promptly deliver to the client or third person any funds or other property that the client or third person is entitled to receive and, upon request by the client or third person, shall promptly render a full accounting regarding such property." Nevertheless, some attorneys are only vaguely familiar with this rule, so the investment agreement should already have language in it to deal with attorney substitutions. Typically, funders require outgoing attorneys to provide a written notice of withdrawal from the case, together with any contact details for new attorneys or law firms. In addition, many investors also require the plaintiff to issue irrevocable instructions to their attorneys as part of the investment agreement, including substituted counsel. These instructions require, among other things, for outgoing attorneys to provide written notice and contact details for new counsel. They also instruct incoming attorneys to abide by the terms of the agreement.

Optimally, the new attorney will agree to cooperate with the terms of the agreement. Usually, however, incoming attorneys will be reluctant to commit to any course of action, especially in writing. At the end of the day, funders may have to convince them that they are responsible for paying them.

Quite often, the attorney may withdraw from a case leaving the plaintiff unrepresented. In such situations, investors should use their best efforts to assist plaintiffs in finding new counsel to get their cases back on track. If the attorney resigned because the claim became impaired, the client will likely have difficulty finding a replacement lawyer and the investment may have to be written off.

Case is Lost, Dismissed, or Resulted in a Nominal Settlement

A variety of circumstances can lead to a complete write-off of an investment. Some cases will inevitably result in no recovery. They may be dismissed on summary judgment, lost at trial or reversed and dismissed on appeal. Others may settle for very low amounts that will be insufficient to pay investors.

When losses do occur, compliance departments must determine what happened to their cases so they may take appropriate measures. Many losses will result as a consequence of uncontroversial factors, without any recourse for investors, and must be simply written off. Others, however, may result from conduct that violates the investment agreement, including malfeasance on the part of the attorney, plaintiff, or both. Certain cases may also be lost because plaintiffs did not cooperate. In these situations, funders may seek to recover their investments from the defaulting parties.

Such an analysis can help investors refine their underwriting methodology by identifying the risks and material events that contributed to the negative outcome. Investors may use this information to strengthen their funding documents, improve their underwriting criteria, and perhaps even conclude to cease investing in certain types of cases.

In claims that resulted in very low settlements, funders will usually require attorneys to furnish copies of settlement agreements and payment instruments like checks and wire transfers to confirm the amount of recovery. If any liens were paid, they will also request an itemized list of liens and proof that those liens were first in line.

Although undesirable, losses present an investor with the opportunity to analyze what went wrong and to implement corrective steps to ensure that similar losses do not recur with future investments.

Payments Monitoring

Another critical role of the compliance team is payments monitoring. As custodians of settlement proceeds, attorneys are responsible for paying all stakeholders. Therefore, the period when attorneys receive payments from defendants at the resolution of disputes is a crucial one for funders. Even if the investment agreement clearly requires them to pay providers before making distributions to their clients or junior lien holders, attorneys often have their own view of regarding how payments should be made. In some situations, particularly tort advances, attorneys may be handling thousands of cases and may have less than perfect record-keeping systems in place. It is critical, therefore, to remind attorneys about their payment obligations to investors and to closely monitor receipt of payments from them.

Collections and Dispute Resolution

The compliance team will also typically engage in collection and dispute resolution when investments default for reasons other than normal attrition, such as losses, dismissals, reversals, and nominal settlements. This may occur due to problematic attorneys who refuse to cooperate with funding agreement terms, or perhaps insist on unreasonable discounts to investor returns. It may also arise when attorneys distribute funds to plaintiffs and other lien holders without paying the funders. It may happen as a result of misrepresentation or even fraud perpetrated by plaintiffs, attorneys, or both.

In these situations, the compliance team will evaluate all of the circumstances to decide on the appropriate course of action. Funders will first perform a cost-benefit analysis to determine if any collection effort is supported by the projected outcome. In many cases, particularly when the investment amounts are small, many companies will elect to write off those investments or agree to significant discounts. In other cases, they may decide to initiate litigation in state or federal court, or most commonly in arbitration. When an attorney's particularly egregious conduct causes a default, providers also have the option of filing bar complaints against counsel in the states where they practice.

Working with Attorneys

The prevailing lawyerly attitude toward legal finance is best characterized as cautious acceptance. Many attorneys understand that legal finance offers significant value, but such financing has not yet reached mainstream status within the legal community.

Tort litigators view consumer advances as a necessary nuisance that may offer their clients peace of mind, enabling them to stay focused on their cases and ending incessant calls to their firm from financially distressed clients pleading for help. Commercial attorneys, particularly those using current-pay or partial contingency models, increasingly view litigation finance as a useful tool to increase business and improve their chances for success. Law firms seeking lines of credit are the most progressive on accepting this industry. They are eager to receive as much money as possible from legal finance lenders.

This value proposition, however, is not apparent to many. For some, the potential benefits may be outweighed by the perceived risks. Besides their natural suspicion of all things new, many lawyers have concerns about how legal finance will change the practice of law. On a macro level, they may be apprehensive about public policy and legal ethics. On a micro level, they might be anxious about how legal finance will impact their practices, perhaps by increasing their workload or their level of liability to clients and unfamiliar third parties. As lawsuit investors seek greater acceptance from the legal profession, they invariably run into a significant number of practitioners who are reticent or even hostile toward legal finance.

There are numerous reasons why attorneys are so wary.

Attorneys are cautious and very protective of their cases and clients. They have invested considerable time and effort to become legal professionals: seven years of school, bar exams and admissions, continuing legal education courses, and years of practice in a demanding and not always lucrative field. Investors are newcomers to this centuries-old process. It should come as no surprise that lawyers tend to be protective of their turf.

From the attorney's perspective, they are the engines that drive the process though a complicated civil justice system. They originate the relationship with the client, investigate the facts and then shepherd all the elements to pursue a claim. In the process, they invest their time, experience and their firm's resources. They do not look favorably at oversight from funders, or having their work scrutinized or criticized, especially by laypersons.

Attorneys are their clients' advocates and must meet certain ethical and professional obligations, lest they risk losing their license to practice law. For example, attorneys cannot share information about cases without their clients' permission, and are understandably cautious about sharing sensitive or privileged information. They will be careful to avoid any conflicts of interest. Those who are cynical about legal finance in general may find the rates charged by funders to be excessive.

Lawyers are concerned about how legal finance transactions will affect them directly. Many are reluctant to take on any additional responsibilities because they are not familiar with the investment process. They may be afraid of getting into regulatory trouble because they do not understand the law relating to legal finance in their state. Moreover, they may be skeptical about the terms of the investment agreement and unwilling to assume any liability if there is a dispute between their client and the funding company.

Still other attorneys maintain busy practices and are reluctant to introduce another level of complexity into their businesses. They may have a policy of not cooperating with funding companies and may even cease representing clients that apply for funding.

Even where attorneys cooperate with the investment process initially, their disposition may change after the investment is made. They may become unresponsive to funders if they feel embarrassed that a claim has yielded a negative outcome. They may seek to reduce the funders' return if pressured to do so by their clients. They may become defensive or antagonistic when they make mistakes like paying other stakeholders before paying funders.

A common problem for funders in this context is the attorneys' demeanor. Lawsuit investors usually work with a particular species of lawyers—the litigators. When complications with the legal finance process arise, litigators are predisposed to taking aggressive measures against their counterparties. They may send contentious correspondence, initiate litigation and even yell and scream at providers' staff to get their way.

While the majority of lawsuit investments are resolved in an amicable and cooperative manner, a sizable minority of cases become contentious as a result of the law firms' aggressive posture toward providers. It may be a refusal to meet their obligations, a request for an unreasonable discount, or the many other things that attorneys conjure up to frustrate an investor's ability to collect. The lawyers' discourteous and uncompromising gambits cause funders to react defensively—often by initiating litigation—which continues to feed the vicious cycle of acrimony. This adversarial process can leave the attorney—who is usually on the losing side of the argument—bitter and resentful toward the entire industry. Sometimes they become liable for violating the terms of the investment agreement, which providers will exploit to recover their investments. As a consequence, these skirmishes, which often affect the attorneys' personal assets, make them less likely to cooperate in future funding requests by their clients, while also causing some to portray legal finance in a negative light.

As the industry expands, both sides should do more to harmonize their relationship. The legal profession must mature in their treatment of funding companies. The truth is that steadfastly courteous lawyers get most of what they want, while those that persist in deception and hardball tactics do not. Funders, on the other hand, should also do more to refine their approach to the legal profession by instilling a culture of cooperation within the industry and by considering more amicable methods of dispute resolution. For example, companies could train their staff to better diffuse contentious situations with law firms. Perhaps an informal and more conciliatory mediation process could resolve many of the current disputes, without adding an unnecessary dose of vitriol into the process.

At the same time, it is always helpful to consider the attorney's role when formulating the investment process and the underwriting methodology. For example, funders should always use their best efforts to:

- *Be courteous.* Funders should always be courteous and professional with attorneys. Most attorneys have no experience with legal finance and may be hesitant to experiment. They will not cooperate with the process if the funder comes off as too pushy, folksy or disrespectful. Some funders who are themselves lawyers should remember that they are not acting in a legal capacity and most attorneys view them as finance companies first.

- *Respect the attorney's time.* Attorneys are busy. When underwriting cases or following up on previous investments, the process should be streamlined to make cooperation from the law firm as simple as possible.

- *Respect the attorney-client relationship.* The attorney is primarily responsible for managing the client and funders should not interfere with this relationship. Issues relating to legal strategy, selecting experts, and negotiating a settlement should be free from undue interference.

- *Built rapport with attorneys and their staff.* Lawyers have numerous assistants and gatekeepers who facilitate their work. These could be receptionists, secretaries, research assistants, investigators or paralegals. In some cases, legal assistants will perform most of the work and may know more about the claims than attorneys. Funders should therefore endeavor to build synergistic and long lasting relationships with attorneys and their staff, which will help facilitate the investment process and perhaps generate new business for the provider.

- *Maintain firm, timely, and clear communication.* Attorneys will often attempt to exploit weakness. When funders procrastinate in communicating their concerns or intentions, or fail to communicate them firmly and clearly, attorneys may interpret that as a sign of weakness. In their communications with law firms, providers must always strike a balance between protecting their own interests and preserving their relationship with the law firm. In many cases, it is usually a good policy to escalate the tone of one's communications gradually, offering the law firm several opportunities to take remedial measures.

- *Trust, but verify.* Attorneys will always know more about their cases than funders. Most attorneys are smart, conscientious and hard-working professionals. However, as with any profession, there are many exceptions. The risk of a disparity of information, therefore, is high, especially in highly technical issues that cannot be properly evaluated without an expert opinion.

Funders should request backup from attorneys for material issues and should also verify them using third-party resources.

Conclusion

As this chapter illustrates, the legal finance investment process consists of four main phases—origination, underwriting, structuring, and compliance—that themselves comprise undertakings, instruments, and strategies of considerable breadth and depth. Origination involves the use of multiple marketing channels to originate deals, attorney referrals, and brokers. Upon reaching an agreement to proceed, underwriters begin a thorough vetting process. Such underwriting ensures that funders receive the return they expect, and that a myriad of potential problems are avoided.

Once underwriting is completed, transaction structuring begins. Structuring centers on the investment agreement, which addresses a variety of circumstances that could arise in the course of the transaction. The primary challenge posed in drafting effective investment agreements lies in striking a balance between the enforceability and flexibility of the document, while keeping its terms attractive to prospective clients and attorneys.

Even after the consummation of a funding transaction, the investment process continues with compliance. Investors and their compliance teams must exercise vigilance in managing their investments for the entire life of the claim. A successful investment process involves thorough preparation, a well-balanced investment agreement, and ongoing monitoring.

One of the most important factors running through all phases of the investment process is a funder's relationships with the attorneys and law firms driving the legal claims. Respecting the attorney's role, the obligations of the attorney-client relationship, and the attorneys themselves—through courtesy, clear communication, and understanding—helps to solidify the working partnership among funder, attorney, and client that lies at the very heart of the investment process.

CHAPTER 5

ADDRESSING THE CRITICISM OF LEGAL FINANCE

Legal finance is not without controversy, having been praised and criticized by legal scholars, practitioners, the media, and special interests on the basis of public policy issues and from a legal ethics perspective. This emerging industry is celebrated by those who welcome it as an equalizer that provides access to the legal system, yet others deride it as a threat to public interest. Lawsuit investors also must contend with a visceral element of suspicion and skepticism; many are opposed to the industry, although they are unsure exactly why.

Critics often do very little to articulate a nuanced argument against legal finance. In the United States, critics generally do not distinguish among the different products that exist in this industry, formulating their arguments as though lawsuit investing were uniform. For example, one major criticism of legal finance is that it wrongfully takes advantage of consumers. This argument may have some relevance in connection with tort advances, which have been criticized as a result of the high fees charged by funding companies, but becomes largely irrelevant in the context of business litigation, which deals with companies rather than individuals. Loans to law firms likewise lack several of the key structural elements that critics detest, but they are often lumped in with other forms of legal finance without any meaningful distinction.

Does Legal Finance Promote Frivolous Litigation?

A leading criticism of legal finance is the suggestion that it leads to increased litigation in society, especially an explosion of frivolous claims and "trafficking" in cases that would otherwise not be filed. This is perhaps the most common and ominous charge leveled at the industry, as it appeals both to the emotions and slippery notions of what might be.

Use of the term "frivolous lawsuit" by legal reformers has frightened the public for decades with images of a legal system run amok, an apocalyptic wasteland of bogus lawsuits brought by wicked lawyers and their greedy accomplices. This caricature, however, is not supported by how the industry operates or the empirical data regarding how lawsuits are filed. Tort advances have been widely available for more than a decade, with more capital available to invest in cases than cases available for investment. And despite their decade-long availability, the anticipated cascade of frivolous litigation has yet to materialize. In fact, we have already seen that the number of tort cases in the United States has actually declined over the past decade.[1] If legal finance actually encourages more litigation, one would expect the opposite result given the proliferation of tort advances during this period. There is also no evidence that total litigation in the United States has increased as a result of legal finance, although such a result may be in the public interest if it were to occur.

But what is the proper level of litigation in society? In *Bates v. State Bar of Arizona*, the Supreme Court said, "We cannot accept the notion that it is always better for a person to suffer a wrong silently than to redress it by legal action."[2] If we believe that greater equality of access to the justice system is a desirable outcome, then an increase in the overall use of courts should be welcomed if it helps finance access to justice for those who cannot afford it unaided. Legal finance, therefore, promotes equilibrium within the justice system by allowing those with legitimate and serious causes of action to enforce their rights. This has the effect of correcting previous distortions in the system that resulted from the scarcity of capital.

Moreover, funders have no incentives to support dubious claims. Consider that investors evaluate lawsuits like venture capitalists evaluate companies—they kick the tires, communicate with the principals, look at documents, and assess the viability of the enterprise—in this case the lawsuit. They make money by winning lawsuits and they lose money when things do not go according to plan.

Most investments are made after a claim has commenced, usually with a legal team already on board. There may be occasional cases that have not yet been filed, which investors may agree to support, but such legal disputes must already be sufficiently advanced for investors to evaluate them. Before they can agree to invest, they must review case documents to understand a claim's prospects for success. For this reason, there is clearly a significant bias toward already-filed cases that have documents for investors to review. In the vast majority of matters, legal finance companies become involved with current or imminent litigation and do not encourage new claims. In fact, all tort advances and most commercial investments relate to claims that are already pending.

But consider a claim that has not yet been filed. If it is inherently frivolous, what would it offer to an investor? It is difficult enough to prevail in excellent cases; why would someone invest in a matter where the chances of victory are minuscule? Interestingly enough, the U.S. Chamber of Commerce, the industry's leading opponent, advances the position that even frivolous lawsuits can make attractive investments, in a paper amusingly titled, "Selling Lawsuits, Buying Trouble."[3] In it, the authors argue that

> although providing non-recourse loans to fund litigation is inherently risky, it does not follow that litigation-finance companies will only finance claims that are likely to succeed. These companies—like all sophisticated investors—will base their funding decisions on the present value of their expected return.... If that potential recovery is sufficiently large, the lawsuit will be an attractive investment, even if the likelihood of

actually achieving that recovery is small. Put simply, the present value (excluding inflation and opportunity cost) of a $500 million claim with only a 10 percent chance of success is still $50 million.[4]

First, contrary to the chamber's assertions, lawsuits with low probabilities of success do not necessarily imply that they are frivolous. Many variables can contribute to a claim's chances of success or failure. It could be that the plaintiff's counsel is not particularly skilled or effective in litigating a particular result. The procedural posture may be daunting or the venue of the dispute may be prejudicial to the plaintiff. Perhaps the most common problem is that there is simply not enough money to afford the costs of the lawsuit. A claim may be strong on the merits, but other factors may diminish its prospects for a favorable outcome. A frivolous case, on the other hand, is one that is meritless.

The chamber's argument is emblematic of the faulty logic that is often employed to condemn legal finance. The authors purportedly assert that merits do not matter: the only thing that matters in lawsuits, they argue, are the alleged damages. However, to accept such a distorted view of legal liability is to ignore the way our legal system operates. In most cases, the actual damages cannot be ascertained until a settlement or verdict is reached; much of the dispute itself will revolve around what damages ought to be. Lawsuits become increasingly contentious and complex as the stakes rise. The size of potential damages is important, but it is far from the only factor that affects case outcomes or the investors' decision to invest in them.

Anyone involved in a lawsuit knows the reality of litigation is a stark contrast to these fast and loose depictions. Great attorneys struggle every day to prevail, even in highly meritorious cases, facing off against talented defense attorneys who are skilled at obstructing them. If the alleged damages in a case are indeed $500 million, but the probability of winning is only 10 percent, when the jury reaches a defense verdict, does the plaintiff still receive $50 million?

Never.

The majority of the time, the plaintiff gets nothing and may even have to pay the defendant's legal expenses, depending on the jurisdiction. What then is a case with a 10 percent probability or even a 50 percent probability of success really worth to a lawsuit investor? The answer is almost invariably zero.

There are many good cases available for investment, with high rates of return, without the risk or stigma associated with frivolous litigation. Constructing a business model predicated on funding frivolous lawsuits, therefore, seems like a terribly difficult way to make a living. There are considerable deterrents to bringing frivolous cases for all the parties involved and it would be rather challenging to create such a dodgy venture, especially on an institutional basis. Plaintiffs risk their reputations (perhaps even criminal sanction if they perjure themselves) and incur a significant opportunity cost by spending several years involved in an exhausting effort that is destined to fail. Attorneys risk their careers by filing frivolous lawsuits and face significant penalties both in state and federal court. Funders with large balance sheets are also risk averse, lest they invite headline risk, regulatory risk, and lawsuits from their aggrieved investors.

Even if we assume, for the sake of argument, that a legal finance investor were devious enough to attempt such an undertaking, he or she would presumably begin with a sober risk analysis. To assume a 10 percent probability of success on a $500 million result is a significant oversimplification of how investments are modeled. Such an analysis would entail probability distributions of achieving a result with the chances of appeal, the cost of the appeal, the chance of succeeding on appeal, and the prospect of a reduction of the result by the court even if the claim were successful. With the potential damages so high, they would also consider the chance of even deep pockets defaulting. Unless such an investment is a pure gamble, our nefarious investor would have to diversify this investment across a pool of many such cases, deploying enormous amounts of capital, much larger than all of the current investments in this industry combined. In reality, however, such deep pools of capital simply do not exist for even great cases, let alone fake ones.

To suggest that an army of such investors is waiting in the wings to spur frivolous lawsuits is of course fiction. There are no incentives to invest money in lawsuits with perilous prospects—and that is exactly what frivolous lawsuits are. In contrast to the claims that legal finance encourages frivolous litigation, it does exactly the opposite: it tends to filter out meritless cases because funders will not take on the risk of such claims.[5]

Some critics are concerned that funding arrangements could adversely affect the settlement process, perhaps causing plaintiffs to refuse settlement for an objectively reasonable amount, and thereby forcing an inflated number of cases to trial. They believe that funding creates an expectation in the plaintiff of a higher award because of the extra expense of legal finance.

The reality is that legal finance actually encourages settlement by depriving financially well-endowed defendants of an unfair advantage. When the wrongdoer realizes that the plaintiff has the resources to pursue a claim, he or she may be compelled to settle the case early to avoid the added expense. Moreover, even when cases do proceed in court, the process should be more streamlined because delay tactics no longer have their intended effect against the plaintiff. From my experience, the evidence points to an increase in the number of plaintiffs refusing to settle for objectively unreasonable amounts, pushing cases to achieve returns which are more closely aligned with the nature of their damages. This does have an effect on settlement outcomes: instead of discouraging settlements overall, it encourages settlements that are more in line with the actual case merits.

Are Tort Advances a Form of Predatory Lending?

From a public policy perspective, several commentators have written about the high costs of tort advances and have drawn parallels with predatory lending. They argue that funding companies charge unreasonably high fees and engage in profiteering by taking advantage of vulnerable consumers who do not understand the terms of the financing arrangements. These critics also dismiss the notion that investing in tort cases is expensive or risky. While these claims have inspired a great deal of vitriol against tort advance companies, they do not survive closer scrutiny.

One critical element of predatory financing that tort advances lack is deception of the consumer. Although plaintiffs will pay more for this type of financing than for traditional loan products, funding companies do not engage in deception during the funding process. Even though this industry, like many others, has had its share of bad operators, most funding companies provide a great deal of disclosure to their clients, in their communications and funding agreements.

There are numerous requirements to provide disclosure to consumers. ALFA best practices, for instance, prohibit deceptive business practices by their members and require disclosure to the consumer.[6] In addition, most of the largest funding companies, which account for the majority of total funding volume, have made their funding agreements more consumer friendly by bringing them in line with the requirements of the New York attorney general in 2005. Funders in New York are required to provide: (a) clear and conspicuous disclosure statements, including the annualized rate of return and the total amount to be repaid, (b) a five-business-day right of cancellation by the client (without penalty), (c) acknowledgment by the plaintiff's attorney that the agreement has reviewed and explained to the consumer, and (d) written translation of the contract for non–English speaking clients.[7] Many funding companies follow the New York disclosure requirements even with consumers from states that do not have analogous disclosure rules.

Claims that consumers are vulnerable, uneducated, or unable to understand the terms of their funding contracts are also misguided. People who receive this type of funding are not disenfranchised, as some critics imply. The majority of clients receiving lawsuit advances are under fifty years old and own their own home.[8] They are also the best informed of any consumer because they are counseled by attorneys who are familiar with their circumstances throughout the entire process—professionals who have an ethical obligation to provide advice to their clients regarding the financing arrangement. This sharply contrasts with how most consumers purchase other financial products, even sub-prime ones. How many credit card applications, mortgage deals, or even payday loans are reviewed by a consumer's attorney?

Most funding providers will agree that legal finance may be an expensive way to raise capital, but they will emphasize that the heavy price tag is directly related to the significant costs of doing business in this industry, which arise from high operating expenses, losses and reductions that accompany such investments, and the overall riskiness of investing in lawsuits. The industry's critics, however, dismiss funding companies' arguments that the high rates of this product are related to the inherent costs and risks of legal finance. They claim the risk is illusory and that investors are able to pick only winners by using sophisticated portfolio models to mitigate risk.

Despite the rose-tinted portrayals of the industry used by critics to impugn funding providers, legal finance businesses are expensive and risky to operate. For companies specializing in tort advances, the average investment is small but the servicing cost is high. Lawsuit advances are very labor intensive to process, but because the average lawsuit advance is less than $5,000, it is hard for investors to achieve economies of scale. The business model for tort deals is hardly the most efficient.

For example, payroll is a big expense for any legal finance provider. Each investment, regardless of size, requires ongoing monitoring, robust systems, staff, collection expenses, and more. Funding companies must hire numerous staff to handle the tasks associated with each and every investment. They require call centers and administrative personnel to handle client records. They need to hire expensive underwriters to review opportunities, as well as collection staff and outside attorneys to deal with cases that run into trouble—as many invariably do. The industry itself does not yet permit a level of automation to effectively contain the costs associated with labor and productivity.

The cost of capital for funding companies is also very high, with providers typically paying annual rates of 12 to 25 percent. The high returns demanded by creditors reflect, among other things, the lack of liquidity and associated risks of non-payment for legal finance instruments. Contrary to the non-recourse nature of lawsuit investments, funding companies typically rely on conventional loans which are full-recourse to the borrower. Thus, even if funding companies lose 30 percent of their underlying cases, they must still repay the full amount of the investment plus interest back to their creditors.

To be fair, it is true that companies in this space attempt to hone their ability to discern winning claimants from those destined to lose. After all, what professional investor would not? What is the purpose of tying up precious company resources in cases bound to be lost? Companies have different underwriting styles, and some have even built complex applications to evaluate opportunities. If done properly, given sufficient investment data, and with adequate diversification, risk can be managed—but never eradicated—on a portfolio basis. Risk, however, cannot be comparably managed on an individual case basis.

Even with the variety of tools available to investors to help manage their investments, legal finance remains a very risky business.

Investments typically occur prior to resolution of the underlying claims, so the prospect of receiving a payment from the defendant is completely speculative. Investment models cannot predict the outcome of any particular claim because just about anything can happen to a lawsuit as it winds its way through an opaque and complicated legal system. There may be an expectation of victory, but the subsequent development of the claim from its inception to final disposition often produces the opposite outcome. Lawsuit investors, then, understandably implement an uncertainty premium that hedges against unforeseeable—and often unavoidable—events.

The argument that tort investments are not risky ignores the realities of the business. As many as 40 percent of all tort advances yield unexpected results, across all case types, including the most promising cases like strict liability claims. Even the most meritorious cases can be lost, dismissed, appealed or abandoned. A very common outcome in litigation is when cases are resolved for just a fraction of the plaintiff's initial demand, forcing investors to accept steep cuts to their returns.

A long investment period and lack of liquidity also contribute to the expense of lawsuit capital. The average tort case takes more than a year to resolve, without the benefit of any interim payments to the funding company to ameliorate risk. There is no established exchange or secondary market for legal finance products, leaving investors with limited ability to exit their investments. They must generally wait for the case to play out before recouping their investment and any realized gain. As a result, the staggered cash flow from cases and lack of liquidity for these products further increase the cost of financing for the plaintiff as investors demand premiums for their capital.

Yet another problem for consumer tort providers lies in third-party liens. Funding companies have no clear visibility of encumbrances on claims that may reduce the amount of settlement proceeds available for distribution from the lawsuit, clouding the priority of payments for all parties. There is no definitive way, for example, for a funder to ensure that plaintiffs are not subject to claims from excessive tax or child support liens (or numerous other statutory liens), which require priority payment and substantially reduce the investor's return. Similarly, providers do not know with any certainty the final amount of any medical liens that must be paid from the proceeds of any settlement, generally because many plaintiffs are still in treatment at the time of funding. Also, many providers cannot know for sure if other companies had previously advanced funds to the same client.

To illustrate the problem, suppose a provider advances $5,000 to a client who was injured in a car accident. The case appears solid on its merits and ultimately settles for $50,000 in 18 months. Let's also suppose that the client owes the funding company $10,000 (principal plus 100 percent interest) from those proceeds. In a perfect world, the distribution would look like this:

› a third or $16,500 goes to the attorney for his time and expertise;

› $10,000 would go to repay the funding company;

› the balance, or $23,500, would go to the plaintiff.

Contrary to this example, however, lawsuit investments are not made in a perfect world. For instance, a funding company has no way of knowing that the plaintiff had a child support lien from another state for $15,000. Medical liens not covered by insurance are an additional $10,000. To further complicate matters, the plaintiff granted his landlord a $5,000 lien against his lawsuit to pay back rent. The client, now angry that he is receiving far less than he expected, instructs his attorney to negotiate everyone down, or even better, not pay them at all if he can figure out a way.

In this scenario, which is not uncommon, the funding company will first have to cede priority to the child support lien, which comes first by law. It will then have to contend with both the medical provider and the landlord to determine who gets paid first.

Because the other lien holders own a bigger piece of the claim, the funding company will likely settle for a much lower return than the contractual obligation would suggest, or perhaps even forfeit the entire amount. Since there are no personal guarantees or further recourse on the part of the plaintiff, the investor has limited options when its ability to collect is impaired by factors which lie outside its control. All of this additional complexity, effort, and expenditure of resources stems from a mere $5,000 investment.

Plaintiffs' attorneys further compound the problem for funding companies. When cases are near resolution or right after they settle, providers will usually send a payoff statement to the client's attorney, indicating the amount due from his client upon resolution of the case. Many attorneys, however, will use every effort to negotiate down the outstanding amount, including using hardball tactics that ultimately lead to collection proceeding against them. This is concern for all lawsuit investors, who have to price their products with this in mind.

Funding companies, therefore, not only experience losses as a result of adverse procedural events like dismissals and defense verdicts; they are also subject to unforeseeable complications that reduce the value of their investments. A substantial portion of their overall portfolio experiences *slippage*, dramatically reducing their blended return.

In reality, legal finance companies specializing in tort advances are not spectacularly profitable. In fact, when factoring in loss rates, discounts, origination costs, salaries and other overhead, many companies barely break even on a cash basis.

Despite their high rates—which are needed to combat the heightened risks involved—lawsuit advances provide a critical service to an underserved community. Even if there are situations where advances consume a large part of the plaintiff's ultimate settlement, the benefit is that plaintiffs receive immediate capital, without risk, which they can use for any emergency. The plaintiff's short-term need for funds may outweigh any negative effect the advance will have on reducing the client's ultimate share of the recovery. On the other hand, perhaps plaintiffs who receive short-term funds will persist in the litigation and receive better results than would have been available if they were forced to settle prematurely. Lawsuit advances give plaintiffs financial options they never had before, giving them the flexibility to monetize their claims if their situation requires it.

Confidentiality and the Attorney-Client Privilege

Other criticisms of legal finance have focused on how this type of financing affects the integrity of civil justice. Some are concerned that because modern legal systems in both civil and common-law countries rely on a complex set of rules and professional ethical obligations to guide legal practitioners, legal finance transactions may have the capacity to compromise these requirements when they come into tension.

Perhaps the most common criticism of legal finance from a legal ethics perspective is regarding its potential to negatively impact the legal profession's duty of confidentiality. Some are concerned that legal finance may undermine the fiduciary and professional obligations of attorneys toward their clients. They argue that confidentiality, the cornerstone of the attorney-client relationship, may be forfeited as a result of disclosures made by attorneys to funding companies while evaluating claims for investment.

The attorney-client privilege is a legal concept that protects certain communications between attorney and client from disclosure to the opposition. In addition, the work-product immunity protects materials prepared by attorneys and third parties in anticipation of litigation from discovery. Under ABA's Model Rule 1.6(a), the attorney is allowed to disclose confidential information to third parties if the client "gives informed consent." There is a great deal of uncertainty about whether the disclosure of privileged communications to a funding provider waives the confidentiality. The court in *Leader Technologies v. Facebook, Inc.* decided that it did, holding that Leader had waived its attorney-client and work-product privilege over the documents it shared with its potential lawsuit investors regarding an opportunity to invest in its patent infringement lawsuit against Facebook.[9] In contrast, two other cases support the view that documents shared with lawsuit investors do not waive confidentiality. In *Mondis Technology, Ltd., v. LG Electronics, Inc.*, a court refused to compel production of documents provided to investors.[10] More recently, in *Devon IT, Inc., v. IBM Corp.*, a claim that was supported by Burford, a court held that discussions with litigation funders are covered by the work-product doctrine.[11] The judge in that case explained that since Burford and Devon share a "common interest" in the outcome of the case and had entered into the confidentiality agreement, their communications were protected.

Although detrimental breaches of confidentiality are possible, a closer examination of how funding companies actually make their investments will reveal that these concerns are overstated. Some may not realize that, in a practical sense, issues regarding the waiver of the attorney-client privilege apply to only a small class of information. The privilege clearly applies only to communications between a client and the attorney, not just any communication about the lawsuit. The client is free to tell a prospective funder anything other than what the client said to the attorney, without waiving the privilege. As a result, the client could tell the funder a great deal, including how the incident came about, so long as the client was not asked what he told his attorney. A funder can examine documents as well, provided they are not communications between the client and the attorney. A prospective investor can expect to receive substantial information from the plaintiff about the claim without ever creating waiver problems.

Providers, therefore, do not require access to sensitive information in the vast majority of deals. In the tort space, the underwriting process is limited in scope and does not generally require disclosure of confidential information. Funding companies tend to focus on police reports, medical treatment records and insurance policy limits—items not subject to either privilege and normally discoverable.

The same is true in most commercial deals and law firm lines of credit. Investors in these types of products can generally evaluate the merits of cases or portfolios of cases without requiring the disclosure of privileged information. They typically examine only documents that are already subject to discovery.

Some commercial investments requiring a more involved underwriting process may, in some cases, need the disclosure of privileged attorney-client work products. In these rare situations, it is possible to structure relationships in a way that avoids any challenges to this privilege. For example, the funding company's attorney can be designated as either the client's agent or co-counsel for purposes of evaluating the merits of the claim by executing a separate legal services agreement. For the client, this would be similar to receiving a second opinion about a case from another lawyer, and any communications between them would therefore remain confidential. Any conflicts of interest arising from representing both the plaintiff and funding company can be waived by the parties. In addition, funding companies can use certain best practices to ensure the privilege is maintained. For example, they can destroy sensitive documents or return them to the disclosing party, without retaining copies. Attorneys aware that a waiver of the privilege is possible upon disclosure of sensitive documents can advise their clients accordingly and take precautions against such a waiver occurring.

Conflicts of Interest

Critics also believe legal finance has the capacity to interfere with another sacred cow of the legal profession: the independent professional judgment of the client's attorney. They suggest that legal finance providers will seek to protect their investments and to maximize the expected value of claims by demanding control over the litigation, perhaps hiring the lawyers directly, devising the litigation strategy to be employed, and deciding whether to accept a settlement offer. From a lawyer's perspective, this may create confusion about who actually owns the claim and controls the lawsuit, also raising questions about how the lawsuit investor's expectations impact the client's best interests.

In arrangements where the investors pay the costs of litigation directly, critics contend that funding companies may exert undue influence over the litigation process, subordinating the plaintiff's interests to those of the lawsuit investor, and perhaps coercing litigants to accept fast and cheap settlements or other undesirable results.

This argument assumes that lawyers need to be protected from overzealous funding companies. It presumes that attorneys are not sophisticated enough to deal with potential conflicts in a professional manner. It makes that presumption despite the fact that there are specific rules requiring attorneys to exercise care against compromising their independent professional judgment, rules that attorneys must learn as a part of passing their state bar exam. Why would these attorneys, fully aware of the professional and ethical obligations owed to their clients, be cowed by the whims of pushy lawsuit investors?

As noted earlier, providers who structure their investments to allow themselves too much control should be rightfully concerned. Courts are not particularly tolerant of funders directing the litigation process and some may even risk being held responsible for the defense costs if they are considered to be too close to the litigation. However, most companies do not attempt to control litigation, and so in most cases there should be no confusion about who the client is. Most transactions in legal finance do not involve the transfer of a cause of action to a new party. They are transfers of only a portion of a claim's proceeds. Moreover, funding companies themselves do not participate in the case in any way and their contracts confer no right of interference. For example, several tort advance companies such as Oasis have gone on the record to explain that their role is purely passive. In the commercial space, two of the largest funders, Juridica and Burford, also confirmed that they do not attempt to control litigation.

Conclusion

As demonstrated throughout this chapter, legal finance has drawn its fair share of controversy. But the arguments advanced against it either rely on inaccurate or baseless assumptions, or herald doomsday repercussions that, by the very nature of the dynamics underlying the legal system and the people who populate it, have not—and are unlikely to ever—come to pass. Ultimately, the reality of legal finance falls more closely in line with its proponents than its naysayers. Legal finance remains a realm of opportunity for claimants to pursue valid claims beyond their own financial bounds, and a fertile ground for investors willing to back worthwhile lawsuits to realize profits commensurate with the risks that they undertake.

CHAPTER 6

REGULATION OF LEGAL FINANCE

L awsuit investors are quick to point out a peculiar aspect of human nature they often encounter in their business: some of their clients are very happy to receive funding but reluctant to pay investors all or part of their contractual obligation once the underlying claim is resolved. In these situations, litigation to resolve the rights of the parties inevitably ensues. It is in this context that courts are asked to opine on the legality of legal finance transactions.

A fair amount of uncertainty lingers around how courts would interpret legal finance deals in a sizable minority of jurisdictions. Despite significant progress in the past decade, the United States still lacks a transparent and comprehensive regulatory regime for legal finance. There is currently no federal law regulating this industry. Rather, the industry is regulated on a state level by a diverse patchwork of case precedent, common law doctrines, state bar ethics opinions, state statutes, and agreements with regulatory bodies. Every state has its own unique perspective of how investment in lawsuits should be treated.

The current state of the law and its application by courts and regulators is very disparate. In the majority of states, legal finance has been allowed to proceed. So far, seven states—Ohio, Michigan, Minnesota, New York, Massachusetts, North Carolina, and South Carolina—have relied upon common law or state usury law to invalidate legal finance arrangements.

Prudent investors must know where state laws permit investing in lawsuits. Since typical tort transactions, as well as a large number of commercial lawsuit investments, are structured as non-recourse assignments of proceeds from plaintiffs to investors, they will also want to know whether the assignment of lawsuit proceeds is permitted in various states. In addition, state usury laws and how a state's courts treat investment models where the payment of proceeds is contingent on the outcome of the claim are important concerns. Since transactions in this industry require the attorneys' blessing, investors will need to determine whether state bar ethics rules allow attorneys to enable and participate in such deals. Finally, providers in this space should be concerned with state licensing requirements, as well as the current legislative and regulatory efforts that may become policy in the states where they invest.

Does State Law Permit Investing in Lawsuits? Maintenance and Champerty Re-examined

A state's interpretation of the doctrines of maintenance and champerty remains an important consideration for lawsuit investors, as they are a favorite defensive argument of recalcitrant clients. These doctrines are contract defenses which may invalidate funding agreements between providers and their funding clients. Some may be surprised to learn that funding agreements have been voided based on champerty in several states. Investors who neglect prevailing maintenance and champerty laws do so at their peril. For example, in *Johnson v. Wright*, the Minnesota Court of Appeals rescinded a funding agreement that required the payment of 27.65 percent of the proceeds from a claim to a third party who was financing the action.[1] Similarly, in *Rancman v. Interim Settlement Funding Corp.*, the Ohio Supreme Court also voided a legal finance agreement on the basis of maintenance and champerty.[2]

In addition, states that seemingly permit investing in lawsuits nevertheless may have restrictions relating to certain types of litigation or the particular form of the investment. Types of investments that are allowed in one state by either case law or statute may nevertheless contravene the law of another state. The absence of dispositive precedent in a jurisdiction does not necessarily mean that a particular type of deal is permitted. It may just be that the opportunity for judicial or regulatory review has never presented itself, until the perfect case comes along.

As a general matter, the modern trend is to allow maintenance and champerty where the arrangements do not clearly offend judicial sensibilities. The former prohibitions against these practices have been significantly relaxed by a growing number of states, provided that certain conditions are met. In fact, as of this writing, Maine, Nebraska and Ohio have passed legislation specifically allowing third-party funding and establishing a regulatory framework for this business.[3]

According to Professor Anthony Sebok, in his seminal article "The Inauthentic Claim,"[4] twenty-eight out of fifty-one jurisdictions permit some form of maintenance. These include Arizona, California, Colorado, Connecticut, Florida, Hawaii, Iowa, Kansas, Louisiana, Maine, Maryland, Massachusetts, Michigan, Missouri, Montana, New Hampshire, New Jersey, New York, North Carolina, North Dakota, Ohio, Oklahoma, Oregon, South Carolina, Tennessee, Texas, Washington, and West Virginia.[5]

Of the twenty-eight states that permit maintenance or champerty in some form, sixteen explicitly allow maintenance for profit (otherwise known as champerty), including Colorado, Connecticut, Florida, Iowa, Kansas, Maine, Maryland, Massachusetts, Missouri, New Hampshire, North Carolina, Ohio, Oklahoma, Oregon, Washington, and West Virginia.[6]

An increasing number of courts have unequivocally declared that their state law permits champerty. In several states—including Arizona, California, Connecticut, Missouri, New Jersey, New Hampshire, New Mexico and Texas—courts have held that common law prohibitions against champerty were never adopted from England. In others, such as Colorado, Florida, Massachusetts and South Carolina, champerty laws were adopted but later rejected.

In *Saladini v. Righellis*, the Massachusetts Supreme Court struck down the state's champerty laws. The court reasoned that "[w]e have long abandoned the view that litigation is suspect, and have recognized that agreements to purchase an interest in an action may actually foster resolution of a dispute." The court also noted that the doctrine of champerty was no longer "needed to protect against the evils once feared: speculation in lawsuits, the bringing of frivolous lawsuits, or financial overreaching by a party of superior bargaining position. There are now other devices that more effectively accomplish these ends."[7]

In Florida, the common law prohibition of champerty was abandoned by an appellate court, which held in *Kraft v. Mason* that no claim of champerty exists unless a stranger to a lawsuit "officiously intermeddles" in the suit.[8]

In *Osprey, Inc. v. Cabana Ltd. Partnership*,[9] the South Carolina Supreme Court abolished champerty as a defense in that state. The court stated that "[w]e are convinced that other well-developed principles of law can more effectively accomplish the goals of preventing speculation in groundless lawsuits and the filing of frivolous suits than dated notions of champerty."[10]

Nevertheless, while the majority of states permit some forms of maintenance and champerty, many still maintain prohibitions against these practices to varying degrees. In New York, for example, courts have taken a nuanced approach to the application of these doctrines. New York is an important state for legal finance because many funding companies are located there, and even those located elsewhere often use New York law in their funding agreements. Moreover, a large number of lawsuit investments also relate to cases being litigated in New York courts, especially larger claims in federal court.

New York's maintenance and champerty laws are relatively permissive, primarily creating problems for agreements entered into before the lawsuit is filed. In situations where the investment is made after the case has been filed, New York courts have been consistently reluctant to invalidate the arrangements based on champerty. Champerty is codified in New York's Judiciary Law § 489, which generally prohibits the purchase of a claim with the intent and for the purpose of bringing a lawsuit, but courts have been reluctant to find actions to be champertous as a matter of law, in large part due to their view that the doctrine has a more narrow application in American jurisprudence compared to its previous use in England. Most of the early cases dealing with champerty in New York were largely directed toward preventing attorneys from filing suit merely as a vehicle for obtaining costs, which is very different from the abuses that existed within the English system.

Consistent with its more narrow view of champerty, the Court of Appeals of New York established a "primary purpose" test for determining whether conduct is champertous. In *Bluebird Partners, L.P. v. First Fidelity Bank, N.A.*, the court explained that the primary-purpose test requires commencing litigation to be a major motivating factor for champerty to apply in any third-party claim transfer.[11] However, the assignment of proceeds in cases, which is the most common model used by lawsuit investors, does not fall within this definition of champerty.[12] In *Grossman v. Schlosser*, the court held that "the assignment of the proceeds of such a cause of action, prior to its settlement or adjudication, [is] valid and effectual as an equitable assignment against the assignor and his attaching creditor, and…such an assignment [is] not against public policy."[13] Recently in *Echeverria v. Estate of Lindner*, a New York court confirmed that the assignment of a portion a lawsuit's recovery does not violate the statute "as long as the primary purpose and intent of the assignment was for some other reason other than bring suit on that assignment."[14]

Still, fourteen jurisdictions continue to maintain a formalist view of maintenance and champerty and explicitly prohibit them. According to Sebok, these include Alabama, Delaware, District of Columbia, Georgia, Illinois, Kentucky, Minnesota, Mississippi, Nevada, Pennsylvania, Rhode Island, South Dakota, Wisconsin, and Virginia.[15]

For example, Delaware still upholds that, under common law, an agreement is champertous whenever an assignee has no interest, either legal or equitable, in a cause of action prior to the assignment. In *Hall v. State*, the Delaware Superior Court noted that champerty "continues to have vitality in this State," and that "[i]t is the duty of this court to dismiss a case in which the evidence discloses that the assignment of the cause of action sued upon was tainted with champerty."[16] Delaware is also an important jurisdiction for legal finance because many companies choose to incorporate there.

Rhode Island also acknowledges maintenance and champerty. In *Toste Farm Corp. v. Hadbury, Inc.*, the Supreme Court of Rhode Island stated "[t]his Court has previously recognized the common law doctrines of maintenance and champerty…although nearly half a century has elapsed since *Martin v. Clarke*, 8 R.I. 389 (1866), the opinion adopting these doctrines], it has never been overruled, doubted or denied, and the same remains the law of the state."[17]

Minnesota has an even stricter view of champerty. In *Johnson*, for example, the Minnesota Court of Appeals examined the common-law history of champerty and stated that "an agreement in which [a party] had no interest otherwise, and when he is in no way related to the party he aids, is champertous and void as against public policy," and that

> [a]lthough there are safeguards in place to alleviate the potential evils associated with champertous agreements, respondent fails to provide a compelling reason to completely abandon the doctrine. As an error correcting court, we do not presume to

abandon the champerty doctrine simply because a few states have chosen to do so.[18]

A minority of states have few, if any, cases dealing with maintenance and champerty. Others have taken largely ambiguous positions as to the current status of their common law relating to these doctrines. For instance, appellate courts in Nebraska, Utah, and Vermont have barely mentioned champerty in the last 100 years. Several others are apparently unsure as to the state of the law in their state. These include Alaska, Arkansas, Indiana, New Mexico, and Wyoming.

It is also important to consider that both the liberal and restrictive rules on maintenance and champerty are distinguishable in numerous ways. It should not be assumed that one model is applicable to multiple jurisdictions. Sebok points out that a number of states have important qualifications in the way they apply their law, even if they otherwise permit maintenance and champerty. For example, Tennessee allows champerty, but not in real estate transactions. Texas, which is known as a liberal jurisdiction for lawsuit investing, nevertheless restricts champerty in certain areas of litigation, like legal malpractice claims.

In addition, certain states place restrictions on the form of maintenance and champerty, with the most common involving limitations on how much control an investor can exercise over the conduct of a claim after an investment has been made. In most states where maintenance and champerty are generally permissible, courts are unlikely to invalidate funding agreements, provided the investor is not: (1) promoting "frivolous" litigation; (2) supporting meritorious litigation motivated by an improper motive; or (3) "intermeddling" with the conduct of the litigation.[19] Several states have invalidated agreements with funders who were perceived as promoting frivolous claims, supporting litigation in bad faith (as a consequence of their personal animosity toward an adversary), or for being too involved in the prosecution of the claim.

There is, unfortunately, no clarity as to how different states would treat varying degrees of control, as there are few cases on point. It is likely, however, that the majority of courts in jurisdictions that do permit maintenance and champerty will be offended by investors' efforts to direct the case in a way that blurs the line between who is the actual party to the claim. This can include efforts to select or direct the litigants' attorneys, to formulate the theory or strategy of the case, or perhaps retain the right to accept or have veto power over a settlement. The structure of any deal, therefore, will greatly affect the application of maintenance and champerty doctrines in each state, and investors should perform an exhaustive review of the law in the relevant jurisdictions to understand the permissible methods of investing there.

Usury

Like maintenance and champerty, usury is a contract defense that can invalidate a funding agreement. In fact, in many states lenders risk losing their principal entirely if the loan is deemed usurious. Because investments in lawsuits do not fit the conventional financial instrument mold, some funding clients (and their lawyers) try to categorize the investments as loans violating the prevailing usury rate, in an effort to escape their obligations under their funding agreement. This logic is sometimes reinforced by tort advance companies, which frequently advertise their services on the Internet as "lawsuit loans."

As previously discussed, usury is receiving interest at a rate that exceeds the maximum rate provided by law for a loan. Usury laws are fairly diverse. There are considerable differences from state to state in the interest rates that constitute usury and the extent to which rates may be specified for different types of lenders (e.g., banks, credit card companies, insurance companies, merchants) and for different types of loans (e.g., personal, commercial, real estate). There are also a number of statutory exemptions from the usury laws in some states, including for business loans, loans above certain threshold amounts (e.g., loans above $250,000), credit card and retail installment debt, as well as penalty interest, first lien mortgage loans, and others. For example, the highest usury rates for consumer loans by statute are in the District of Columbia and Maryland at 24 percent, while the lowest is in Michigan at 7 percent. The usury rate in New York for consumer transactions is 16 percent. A handful of states, including Nevada and New Hampshire, have no usury caps.

Courts do not generally favor a finding of usury. In most states the burden of proof is on the party asserting it. In New York, for instance, "usury must be proved by clear and convincing evidence as to all its elements and will not be presumed."[20] However, a finding of usury cannot be avoided simply by categorizing a transaction as something other than a loan. Courts will look through the form of the deal to determine if it is a loan in substance.

Generally speaking, the usury defense is relevant almost exclusively in tort transactions because commercial investments tend to be exempt from usury either due to the size of the investment or because the investment is received by a business rather than an individual consumer. Most states exempt one or the other category from their usury laws. In many other commercial deals, usury is not relevant because the transactions are structured as outright purchases of an asset, perhaps a patent or even a direct investment into the equity of a company that is involved in litigation.

In the tort advance context and in commercial investments that cannot avail themselves of a statutory exemption from usury laws, investors rely on an implicit assumption that investments in lawsuits (other than loans to law firms) are not loans at all, but rather ownership interests in a contingent asset. They contend that usury laws do not apply to them because one of the elements of usury —an absolute obligation to repay the sums advanced—is missing. The contemporary debate over whether lawsuit investments are loans subject to usury has focused on this assumption. This argument has been widely accepted by state courts, although several jurisdictions have advanced an important limitation to this rule.

In *Dopp v. Yari*, a New Jersey District Court rejected the usury defense, holding that a loan for which repayment depends upon a contingency cannot be considered usurious.[21] The Florida District Court of Appeal came to the same conclusion in *Kraft*. In *Anglo-Dutch Petroleum Int'l, Inc. v. Haskell*, the Texas Court of Appeals also supported this theory.[22] But the *Anglo-Dutch* court went even further. In that case, which was a commercial investment syndicated to a number of investors, the funding client argued that when it entered into the funding agreement there was no real risk it would lose the underlying lawsuit because it was already conclusively established by documentary proof that the defendants were liable. The funding client argued that investors were almost certain to recoup their money and the investment's repayment was, therefore, absolute. The court rejected this distinction, noting that the terms of the agreement specifying the contingent nature of the transaction was enough to exempt it from state usury laws.[23]

In New York, the non-recourse exemption from usury is well settled. For example, the New York County Supreme Court in *The Matter of Lynx Strategies LLC v. Ferreira* confirmed the holding of the 1936 case *O'Farrell v. Martin*: "[w]hen payment or enforcement rests on a contingency, the agreement is valid though it provides for a return in excess of the legal rate of interest."[24] In *Ferreira*, a tort advance provider brought a motion to confirm an arbitration award against a law firm and its client. The court granted the plaintiff's petition, holding that

> a defense of usury is not applicable to the matter herein. The concept of usury applies to loans, which are typically paid at a fixed or variable rate over a term. The instant transaction, by contrast, is an ownership interest in proceeds for a claim, contingent on the actual existence of any proceeds. Had respon-

dent been unsuccessful in negotiating a settlement or winning a judgment, petitioner would have no contractual right to payment. Thus, usury does not apply to the instant case.[25]

Recently, in *Kelly, Grossman & Flanagan, LLP v. Quick Cash, Inc.*, the Suffolk County Supreme Court confirmed the reasoning in *Ferreira*, holding

> [s]imilarly, here, the transactions between the parties create ownership interests in proceeds of claims, contingent on the actual existence of any proceeds. Plaintiffs would have no contractual right to payment had [d]efendants been unsuccessful in negotiating settlements or winning judgments in the underlying actions. Therefore, under the circumstances, usury does not apply.[26]

Not all courts, however, agree that the contingent nature of transactions provides a safe harbor for all lawsuit investments. Several courts have required the risk of loss relating to the underlying lawsuit investment to be genuine and not illusory. In *Echeverria*, for example, the court held that when the risk of non-recovery is virtually non-existent, a lawsuit advance should be treated as an absolutely repayable loan.[27] In *Rancman*, the appellate court affirmed a lower court's holding that lawsuit advances were absolutely repayable where the risk that plaintiff would fail to recover in the underlying lawsuit was virtually non-existent.[28] In *Lawsuit Financial, LLC v. Curry*, the Michigan Court of Appeals affirmed a lower court summary judgment ruling on usury grounds because little or no risk of non-recovery existed in the funding transaction.[29] The court stated:

> We believe that the transactions at issue here were loans because at the time the advances were made, plaintiff had an absolute right to repayment. In support of its argument that plaintiff did not have an absolute right to repayment, plaintiff directs us to language in the agreements that states that repayment is contingent on defendant Curry's recovery. Despite that language in the agreements, we conclude that the right to repayment was absolute

because the parties entered into those agreements long after the defendants in the underlying personal injury suit admitted liability and after the jury returned a verdict of $27 million in damages.[30]

The *Curry* decision serves as a warning to providers to make sure their investments truly have risk, rather than just the appearance of risk. Investors should be careful when funding cases where there is no possibility of non-payment or where the contingency has already occurred, which is not generally a significant problem for most funding companies because the prospect of recovery in the overwhelming majority of cases is far from certain. Even settled cases where liability is admitted have many risks that can impact the ultimate recovery of funds.

A recent ruling by the Denver District Court in *Oasis Legal Finance v. Suthers* poses a much more serious concern for funders.[31] In that case, LawCash and Oasis, two major national tort advance providers, sued the Colorado attorney general to obtain a declaratory judgment holding that their activities are not loans within the meaning of Colorado's Uniform Consumer Credit Code. The providers' principal argument was that the transactions did not violate the statute because they were contingently repayable and did not constitute loans. The court disagreed, holding that under Colorado's Uniform Consumer Credit Code, debt need not be recourse and consumer tort advance transactions made with an "expectation of repayment" cannot charge more than the interest permitted by the state's usury law.[32]

The Oasis decision, while clearly a minority position, raises the specter of similar interpretation in jurisdictions where consumer legislation is comparably broad and where regulators are seeking means to regulate the industry.

As with maintenance and champerty, lawsuit investors—particularly those involved in tort transactions—must remain mindful of the prevailing usury rate, lest applicable laws deprive them of their entire principal. While courts do not generally favor findings of usury, placing the burden of proof on the party asserting it, merely categorizing a transaction as something other than a loan is by itself insufficient to avoid a finding of usury. Contemporary debate over the application of usury to lawsuit investments has focused on the absolute obligation to repay the sums advanced as the critical element of usury that is absent from lawsuit investments. While the distinction has been widely recognized by state courts, prudent investors should acquaint themselves with the important exceptions advanced by several jurisdictions.

Unconscionability and Contracts of Adhesion

The contract defense of unconscionability has been another defensive weapon of clients who have sought to challenge the validity of funding agreements. Unconscionability is a matter of state law reflecting general fairness concerns. Unconscionable agreements offend notions of fair play and are so one-sided as to render them unenforceable. This doctrine is primarily applicable to consumer transactions but there are occasional commercial applications. If a court finds unconscionability, it may refuse to enforce the entire agreement, refuse to enforce a part of the agreement it deems to be unconscionable, or perhaps limit the application of an unconscionable provision to avoid an unconscionable result.

Again, like the previous defenses, the unconscionability argument usually arises when a client's lawyer seeks a discount. They may reach back to their law school days and say something like, "This contract is unenforceable...it is unconscionable...it is a contract of adhesion!" But what does this really mean?

Without further background regarding the circumstances of the transaction, this statement is meaningless. Unconscionability is often asserted in the context of form contacts, also known as "contracts of adhesion." Most contracts in modern business are indeed form contracts and there is nothing inherently wrong with them. In a typical legal finance deal, only a few terms, like price or the amount and timing of funding, perhaps also the scope of the attorney's involvement, may be negotiated on a deal-by-deal basis, while the preconceived boilerplate usually specifies the remaining obligations of the parties.

Contract law permits the enforcement of form contracts and allows the drafting party—almost always the seller in consumer contracts and often the buyer in commercial contracts—a great deal of latitude to customize the law that will govern its transactions. Generally speaking, most courts will enforce the terms contained in such agreements if the non-drafting party indicates his general acceptance of the form, regardless of whether that party approved all the terms, understood those terms, has read them, or even has any idea what they mean. There are limited exceptions to this rule, most notably if the terms are found to be "unconscionable."[33]

Unconscionability may be procedural or substantive. In most jurisdictions both must exist for a finding of unconscionability. Procedural unconscionability may arise because of wide disparity between the provider and the funding client. It may occur as a result of dramatically uneven bargaining power, which frequently occurs when one party is sophisticated and the other is not, perhaps as a result of education, intelligence, cultural factors, or other reasons that create a significant knowledge asymmetry between the contracting parties. Other concerns may relate to the way the contract is drafted. Agreements that are not completely filled in or are easily altered are susceptible to abuse and therefore viewed by courts with suspicion.

Courts and state regulators have also considered whether the contract is drafted in a way that is accessible to the average consumer. For example, a number of states—including Connecticut, Minnesota, New York and Pennsylvania—have "plain English" laws that require consumer contracts to be written in simple and understandable language. In addition, lawmakers have required providers to furnish agreements in the client's native language where one of the parties is a non-native English speaker.[34]

Suggestions of procedural unconscionability in legal finance transactions are in reality misplaced. It is difficult to imagine any consumer that is better counseled with respect to a financial transaction than a legal finance client. Few consumers of financial products, including small businesses, have the benefit of an attorney to advise them regarding their purchases. Even in real estate closings, attorneys rarely opine on the suitability of mortgage agreements. Yet legal finance clients have the benefit of legal counsel throughout the entire process, including the negotiation of the terms of the funding agreement, the pendency of their claim, and at the time of payment.

Substantive unconscionability concerns the contractual terms themselves, requiring a determination of whether they are commercially reasonable and not "so oppressive that no reasonable person would make them and no fair and honest person would accept them."[35] What specifically amounts to substantive unconscionability to judges is not clear. There are few cases where courts precisely outline these elements. It seems that a combination of factors motivates a finding of unconscionability. In consumer transactions, exorbitant pricing, for one, can arouse the passions of jurists. Another contentious requirement is the use by funders of mandatory arbitration as a dispute resolution forum.

In *Fausone v. U.S. Claims, Inc.*, the plaintiff raised unconscionability as a defense to an action by a tort advance provider to enforce its contract.[36] After the plaintiff prevailed in her underlying lawsuit, she refused to pay U.S. Claims, which initiated arbitration in Philadelphia. Thereafter, she filed a petition for declaratory judgment in Florida, arguing that the terms of her agreement with U.S. Claims were unconscionable, that she was being charged usurious interest, and that she should not be compelled to arbitrate.

U.S. Claims was awarded $72,117 in arbitration. The plaintiff then filed to vacate the arbitration award in Florida, which was denied by the trial court. On appeal, the Florida District Court of Appeal acknowledged that legal finance agreements are not treated like consumer loans, refusing to entertain any usury arguments and affirming the trial court's enforcement of the arbitration decision.[37] However, the court noted that "[t]he purchase agreement in this case is one-sided and designed to prevent a Florida citizen from having access to a local court or another local dispute resolution forum."[38]

In recent years, the validity of mandatory arbitration clauses found in most legal finance agreements, which requires that any legal claim arising from the contract be pursued through private arbitration rather than litigation in state or federal court, has been a subject of controversy.[39] Courts had historically resisted enforcing arbitration clauses, as they perceived arbitration to be an encroachment on their power, until Congress passed the Federal Arbitration Act in 1925 to reverse this attitude and put arbitration agreements on the same footing as contracts generally. Since then, most courts have upheld the enforceability of arbitration clauses, and the ones that have been struck down now have to contend with the Supreme Court ruling in *Buckeye Check Cashing, Inc. v. Cardegna*.[40]

In that case, the Supreme Court confirmed the validity of mandatory arbitration provisions, ruling that arbitration supersedes state law and that arbitrators may decide all issues, including the legality of the contract, unless the arbitration clause was itself challenged. The opinion by Justice Antonin Scalia explained that "unless the challenge is to the arbitration clause itself, the issue of the contract's validity is considered by the arbitrator in the first instance."[41]

In a practical sense, all determinations relating to champerty, usury, and assignability in legal finance agreements can only be made in arbitration and not state or federal court. When a party resisting arbitration argues that it never entered into an agreement at all—perhaps if it did not sign the agreement or lacked legal capacity to consent—courts may first have to determine whether there is an agreement to arbitrate before a dispute can be sent to arbitration.

This, however, does not give lawsuit investors *carte blanche* in arranging relationships with their clients. It is not clear, for example, if unconscionability arguments should be dealt with in court or in arbitration. Similarly, an arbitrator can find any contract defenses to be as persuasive as any court would. To guard against a finding of unconscionability in consumer transactions, investors should implement a set of best practices in their relationships with their clients.

To mitigate the risk of unconscionability, providers should clearly explain the terms of their agreements to their customer in language that is unambiguous to them, preferably in their native language. Funding agreements should provide a clear explanation of the rates being charged, itemized for the amount of money advanced to the recipient. Investors should refrain from overfunding cases by providing only an amount that both the case and the plaintiff can sustain under the circumstances. Moreover, plaintiffs should be afforded a cooling-off period during which the consumer can cancel the agreement without obligation.[42]

In the end, unconscionability is another defensive weapon with which lawsuit investors should be prepared to contend. Unconscionability can be procedural—arising from a disparity of power between provider and funding client or the accessibility of the contracting language—or substantive—concerning the contractual terms themselves—with some courts requiring that both be shown. A set of best practices in relationships with clients may be a lawsuit investor's greatest safeguard against a finding of unconscionability.

Assignment

Assignment is the transfer, in whole or in part, of one person's rights or property to another. Many legal finance deals, both consumer and commercial, are structured as purchase and sale transactions. Assignments in legal finance can take on different forms. In some cases, they may require the transfer of the entire lawsuit asset to the investor, as in matters where investors purchase a patent and then attempt to monetize it, perhaps by filing an infringement lawsuit. They may arise in the context of purchasing judgments against debtors or where a cause of action (right to sue) is assigned to a third party. In these instances, the buyer steps "into the shoes" of the seller who originally had the right to bring the lawsuit. Assignments in legal finance, however, most commonly come about when recipients assign only a portion of their prospective lawsuit proceeds to funders to secure their purchase. For this reason, it is important for lawsuit investors to consider to what extent state law (and in some cases federal law) permits the assignment of claims and proceeds from recipients to investors.

Like champerty and maintenance, many states have limitations on assignments relating to lawsuits. In fact, many states limit assignment precisely because of maintenance and champerty, namely because of concerns relating to undue influence and the exercise of control by third parties over litigation. These concerns are emblematic of the raging debate in the United States about whether lawsuits ought to be treated like property and subject to commercialization like most other forms of property.

Assignment of Causes of Action

When plaintiffs assign their causes of action, for example the right to sue for breach of contract, they lose all control over the litigation, including formulation of the litigation strategy, the right to hire and fire counsel, and all aspects relating to the settlement of the claim. The early common law prohibited all assignments of a cause of action, regardless of its nature. As with maintenance and champerty, however, these restrictions have over time been relaxed or superseded by statute and case precedent. The modern view is that most causes of action are assignable, subject to a number of specific exceptions.[43] In *Osuna v. Albertson*, a California Court of Appeal explained that "assignability of things [in action] is now the rule; non-assignability, the exception; and this exception is confined to wrongs done to the person, the reputation, or the feelings of the injured party."[44] For example, the assignment of personal torts, including personal injury, defamation, assault and battery, false imprisonment, malicious prosecution, invasion of privacy, conspiracy and unfair and deceptive trade practices is generally not allowed. In *Horton v. New South Ins. Co.*, for example, a North Carolina appellate court found the assignment of a plaintiff's interest in a personal tort claim to be void as against public policy because it promoted champerty.[45]

Perhaps the most important exception is that the assignment of causes of action for personal injury is prohibited in nearly every state.[46] Similarly, professional malpractice (medical and legal) actions are not assignable in most states.

Fraud causes of action are assignable in many, but not all states. For example, fraud claims are assignable in fourteen states: Colorado, Illinois, Iowa, Maryland, Michigan, Minnesota, Mississippi, Nebraska, New York, South Dakota, Texas, West Virginia, Wisconsin, and Wyoming. Seven states have taken the opposite position, entirely prohibiting the assignment of fraud claims. These include Georgia, Kansas, Massachusetts, Nevada, New Jersey, Oklahoma, and Vermont. Eleven states have taken the position that assignability of fraud claims turns on whether it arose out of a personal injury or an injury to property. These are Alabama, California Connecticut, Florida, Idaho, Missouri, North Dakota, North Carolina, Virginia, Utah, and Washington. The remaining states probably allow assignment for fraud claims, but do not have any case precedent for fraud.[47]

Assignment of Proceeds from Claims

There is an important distinction in the law of assignment. When a cause of action is transferred to a third party, the original plaintiff ceases to be the owner of that claim and the new owner assumes all the rights and title to prosecuting that claim. This is illustrated in the following example: imagine that my car is damaged by a neighbor, and I sell my right to sue the neighbor to a friend for $50. Such an outright transfer is a rare structure for legal finance transactions because the participation of the plaintiff is usually central to the prosecution of the claim. In legal finance, the majority of assignments occur where there is a sale of only a portion of the plaintiff's future proceeds from the claim, not the plaintiff's very right to sue as in the preceding example. In an assignment of proceeds, I would sue the neighbor directly, but transfer the first $100 out of any future recovery to my friend for an immediate payment of $50.

Most proceeds from claims are assignable. Even proceeds from personal torts like defamation and personal injury are assignable in many states. Subject to several exclusions, any state which has adopted the Revised Article 9 of the Uniform Commercial Code (UCC) now permits the assignment of proceeds from personal torts, including personal injury claims, while still prohibiting assignment of causes of action in those claims.[48]

New York, for example, permits the assignment of the proceeds of personal injury suits. Conversely, twenty-one states still prohibit the assignment of even a portion of the proceeds from personal injury cases (and perhaps other personal tort claims as well). These include Arizona, Arkansas, Colorado, Connecticut, Florida, Illinois, Indiana, Kentucky, Maine, Massachusetts, Minnesota, Mississippi, Missouri, Montana, New Jersey, New Mexico, Pennsylvania, South Dakota, Tennessee, Washington, and Wisconsin.[49]

State limitations on assignment do not mean those states are off limits to lawsuit investors. If there are no other prohibitions or regulatory impediments, providers have generally relied on alternate contract principles to structure transaction in states that do not permit assignment. In tort and some commercial deals, providers have relied on basic contract principles (i.e. the creation of a promise to pay) to create enforceable liens on the proceeds of any recovery. Commercial funders have also taken equity stakes in companies that are litigating in these jurisdictions, which do not require an assignment.

Although once prohibited at common law, an assignment of causes of action is today subject to several specific exceptions. Among these exceptions are the assignment of personal torts and professional malpractice causes of action. Seven states do not allow the assignment of fraud claims; fourteen do. The assignability of fraud claims for the remainder likely depends on the situation from which the claim arose. Unlike an assignment of causes of action, the assignment of proceeds from claims does not remove the plaintiff from participating in the prosecution of the claim. Most proceeds in this context are assignable, even for personal torts, particularly in jurisdictions that have adopted the Revised Article 9 of the UCC. While some states place limitations on the assignability of proceeds from certain types of claims, alternative contract principles can nevertheless be used to create enforceable funding agreements. Thus, the safety of the assignment of causes of action or proceeds by lawsuit investors depends most heavily on the jurisdiction in which the assignment will occur.

Regulation of Attorneys

The attorney is a critical component of any lawsuit investment. His or her participation and cooperation is essential at every stage of the process. Every state has adopted rules governing lawyer conduct and every state has instituted some form of disciplinary body to enforce those rules. In addition, almost every state has a bar association that issues ethics opinions to help its members interpret those rules. Depending on the state, ethics opinions may be advisory, persuasive or binding in nature. Attorneys usually rely on ethics opinions to guide their conduct with respect to issues that are not particularly well settled.

In virtually every state, the rules governing lawyer conduct are based on model standards developed by the American Bar Association, which remains active in shaping attorney conduct by issuing ethics opinions.

Consistent with the ABA's Model Rule 1.8, many state bar ethics opinions have generally tolerated legal finance transactions, provided attorneys fulfill certain disclosure requirements and avoid conflicts of interest. For example, attorneys are allowed to share information about cases with investors after receiving the client's consent. Moreover, they are allowed to honor a client's written assignment or lien for a portion of the proceeds from a recovery. The New York City Bar Association had recently recognized the growth of legal finance and commented that it is a "valuable means for paying the costs of pursuing a legal claim, or even sustaining basic living expenses until a settlement or judgment is obtained." However, state ethics opinions in Connecticut, New Jersey, Missouri, Maryland and Pennsylvania require attorneys to warn their clients about a possible loss of attorney-client privilege when making disclosures to providers.

So far, twenty-nine jurisdictions have issued ethics opinions relating to legal finance. Those jurisdictions are Alaska, Arizona, California, Colorado, Florida, Georgia, Illinois, Kentucky, Maine, Maryland, Massachusetts, Michigan, Missouri, Montana, Nebraska, Nevada, New Jersey, New York, North Carolina, Ohio, Pennsylvania, South Carolina, Tennessee, Texas, Utah, Virginia, Washington, Washington DC, and Wisconsin.[50]

Regulatory Efforts

Many of the regulatory efforts in this space are a result of perceived abuses in consumer transactions by tort advance providers, primarily as a response to the high rates charged by the funding companies. Indeed, tort advances have been very expensive from their inception and rates remain quite steep even today. Even if the high rates are not driven by profiteering, but simply reflect the high costs (and commensurate risks) of doing business in this space, quite frequently they have the capacity to consume a significant part of the plaintiff's ultimate recovery if not properly structured, especially if the underlying cases do not resolve as expected. While most courts have come to accept that the non-recourse nature of most legal finance transactions exempts them from usury laws, several states have considered the impact of the industry and have attempted various efforts at regulation and even outright prohibition.

The industry's first brush with regulation occurred in New York in 2004, when activist Attorney General Elliot Spitzer began to investigate tort advance providers after receiving several consumer complaints. The investigation found that providers were neither skirting lending laws nor misleading consumers, and that lawsuit advances were properly exempt from usury. Following the investigation, several companies who were members of the newly formed American Legal Finance Association entered into a voluntary agreement with the New York attorney general to make their business practices more consumer friendly.

The next battle occurred in Texas in 2005, where Anglo Dutch Petroleum, a commercial recipient of lawsuit funding, that was sued by legal finance companies to enforce a funding agreement, initiated an effort to outlaw the industry by convincing Texas lawmakers to introduce a bill to prohibit legal finance in that state. They almost succeeded, but ALFA was able to defeat the bill in the eleventh hour. Several investor groups ultimately prevailed against Anglo Dutch, creating a landmark precedent for the industry in Texas.[51]

In Maine, a law allowing legal finance was enacted in 2008. Thereafter, in an effort to supersede the Rancman decision that effectively prohibited legal finance in Ohio, ALFA successfully lobbied to enact legislation specifically authorizing legal finance in that state, which also became law in 2008. Nebraska followed suit in 2010.

At the same time, however, Illinois, Maryland, and Colorado require funding companies to register as lenders. Oasis, the largest tort advance provider, paid a $105,000 fine in Maryland for its activities in that state. Illinois has issued cease-and-desist orders to companies operating in that state without a license.

Recently, legal finance has come under increasing attack in individual state legislatures and, to a lesser extent, by state regulatory agencies. This is reflective of an escalating assault on the industry initiated and maintained by an informal alliance between the U.S. Chamber of Commerce and the insurance lobby. Both believe they have an interest in fighting legal finance, as they perceive that it leads to larger and more expensive results which, in turn, costs their memberships more money in legal fees and expenses.

To date, the most effective tool in combating lobbyists and the chamber has been ALFA. As borne out below, ALFA has been remarkably successful in combating proposed legislation antithetical to industry interests. Despite these achievements, many providers want to adopt a separate and less rigorous set of protections.

The following paragraphs detail the legislative and/or regulatory issues of various jurisdictions. Additionally, investors should be aware that although many pieces of legislation may have been recently defeated or delayed, many will—most likely—be reintroduced in the near future.

Recent State-Level Regulatory Efforts

The state-level regulatory landscape remains largely uncertain for legal finance. Several states have introduced bills that would establish basic frameworks and consumer protections. In Alabama, Arizona, Arkansas, Connecticut, Indiana, Kentucky, and Tennessee, those bills were killed in their respective legislative sessions, often as a result of ALFA's efforts against unfairly negative legislation. In other states, notably New York and Texas, the status of those bills remain in perennial limbo. Many of the failed bills sought to impose fee, rate, or time caps, set licensing requirements for funding companies, or restrict the use of arbitration in resolving disputes stemming from legal finance agreements. Some, like Indiana's failed House Bill 1274, would have blurred the distinction between traditional loans and legal finance.

Maryland in particular has a rigorous licensing requirement, which would place any non-licensed funders doing business in its jurisdiction in the state's crosshairs.

Some recent cases, including a 2008 federal bankruptcy case in Kentucky and the now-infamous *Odell* decision in North Carolina, found funding agreements to be usurious under their respective state laws. As a result of these decisions, legal funders operating in Kentucky or North Carolina run the risk of potentially having their investments voided.

Other states have seen their respective offices of the attorney general or other regulatory bodies seek action against legal funding companies. The Colorado attorney general's office in particular has litigated against legal finance companies, arguing that the companies' offerings are technically loans, and thus bound by the Colorado law that requires the licensing of lenders offering loans with APRs in excess of 12 percent. In Nevada, the Department of Business and Industry, Financial Institutions Division (NDBI) investigates funding companies that receive a consumer complaint. As of this writing, the Nevada attorney general's office is also taking a hard look at the legal finance industry. Until efforts between ALFA, the NDBI, and the attorney general's office culminate in an agreement, investing in Nevada cases will continue to represent significant risk.

Conclusion

The regulation of legal finance remains fraught with uncertainty. Although significant progress has been made in the past decade through the efforts of industry advocacy groups like ALFA, the United States still lacks a transparent and comprehensive regulatory regime for legal finance. Those calling for regulation fail to recognize that their money may be better spent elsewhere: the size of the tort advance industry is minuscule compared to the size of the legal sector, making its impact on insurance companies negligible. Ironically, the controversy, which has to a great extent been invented by overzealous lobbyists, has convinced members of both the Chamber of Commerce and insurance companies—many of whom are potential plaintiffs who actually stand to benefit from legal finance—that legal finance companies somehow pose a threat.

With no federal law to guide the industry, regulation has fallen to the states, which have used a patchwork of case precedent, common law doctrines, state bar ethics opinions, statutes, and regulatory body agreements. Each state correspondingly has its own unique view of how investment in lawsuits should be treated. The degree of regulation—or whether lawsuit investments are permitted in a state at all—varies greatly among jurisdictions.

Potential investors in commercial legal finance should also consider the following. The efforts to regulate legal finance described above relate specifically to the activities of tort advance providers, as few commercial funding deals have thus far been tested in court or examined by state lawmakers due to their relative novelty. Companies specializing in commercial deals often attempt to cultivate a rarefied, institutional image, because they are wary of any imputed stigma associated with tort advance companies. To this end, they go out of their way to distinguish themselves from tort providers and even stay away from ALFA or any lobbying efforts to make legal finance more accepted in the United States. What those companies fail to realize is that most lawmakers simply do not appreciate the distinction. As a result, the majority of legislative proposals to date have not sought to exclude commercial transactions from their regulatory reach.

However, there are indeed significant differences between commercial legal finance and tort advances. Businesses are sophisticated players and investments in this space are often in the millions of dollars. Ultimately, commercial legal finance companies must get involved in the legislative discourse or risk being regulated in the same way as tort advance providers.

CHAPTER 7

LEGAL FINANCE IN OTHER COUNTRIES

The assent of legal finance is truly an international phenomenon. There have been funding transactions in Australia, Canada, Germany, Hong Kong, Singapore, South Africa, and the United Kingdom, among others. Most countries in Europe, for instance, including civil law jurisdictions, permit third parties to fund litigation.[1]

The majority of the financing activity in this space, however, is concentrated in common law countries, which also have to contend with many of the same problems the United States faces, namely the high costs of litigation that impede access to justice. For example, according to the recent Oxford Study,[2] the joint costs of pursuing a large scale damage case with damages of $6 million to full trial in English and Welsh courts were estimated at $3 million or 50 percent of the value of the claim.[3] According to the study, the legal costs of suing in England and Wales, a common law jurisdiction, were 30 times greater than in Germany, a civil law jurisdiction.[4] In addition, unlike the United States, most common jurisdictions following the English rule have to contend with fee-shifting laws that require the losing party in a lawsuit to cover the legal expenses of the prevailing party, which also has the undesirable effect of reducing access to justice.

Of all common law countries, legal finance has been most enthusiastically embraced in Australia and United Kingdom. Almost all financing transactions in this space relate to commercial disputes as tort litigation is not as common. In a typical deal, the funder pays all the costs of the claim and usually indemnifies its client against the risk of paying the other party's costs if the claim is lost. In return, if the claim is successful, the funder will receive a percentage of any funds recovered by the plaintiff, usually one-third of the proceeds.

Although possessing noteworthy dissimilarities, the legal systems of Australia and the United Kingdom share with the U.S. legal system a common lineage formed by English common law. Examining the ways in which the legal finance industry has burgeoned in Australia and the United Kingdom—two jurisdictions that view the legal finance industry from more supportive legal standpoints than the United States—sheds light on both the prospects for investors operating in those jurisdictions, and how attitudes toward legal finance in the United States might evolve to become equally supportive.

Australia

In the past decade, Australian courts have emerged as thought leaders of legal finance. Their progressive views have outpaced the development of the industry in other countries by a large margin. Legal finance, or litigation funding as it is known in Australia, has thrived for nearly two decades despite numerous challenges to its legality. Between 1999 and 2007, detractors have challenged third-party funding arrangements twenty times, but no case has ever been invalidated because of the existence of a funding agreement. Litigation funding in Australia has endured.

The Australian legal finance industry arose mainly out of the statutory exception for insolvencies, enabled by the Corporations Act and Bankruptcy Act providing external controllers and trustees in bankruptcy with statutory powers of sale. In Australia, insolvency practitioners, in the same context as bankruptcy trustees in the United States, have exercised their statutory powers to sell a portion of future lawsuit proceeds in return for funding the litigation. The insolvency context was seen as an exception to the rules against maintenance and champerty, which also remained on the books in Australia since colonial days. As judicial attitudes towards maintenance and champerty relaxed and greater access to justice became more desirable, some companies expanded the market by investing in cases outside of the insolvency scenario. As in other common-law countries, by this time Australian courts acknowledged that maintenance and champerty were largely outdated doctrines.

The New South Wales Law Reform Commission observed that "the considerations of public policy which once found maintenance and champerty so repugnant have changed over the course of time. The social utility of assisted litigation is now recognized and the provision of legal and financial assistance viewed favourably as a means of increasing access to justice."[5] Maintenance and champerty were abolished by statute as crimes in New South Wales, Australia's most populous state.

Some courts have even gone so far as to welcome third-party funding of lawsuits. For example, in *QPSX Ltd. v. Ericsson Australia Pty. Ltd.*, the court explained that due diligence and formulation of litigation budgets by firms like IMF (Australia) Ltd. injects "a welcome element of commercial objectivity into the way in which such (complex commercial litigation) budgets are framed and the efficiency with which the litigation is conducted."[6]

The seminal case in Australia relating to litigation funding is *Campbells Cash and Carry Pty. Limited v. Fostif Pty. Ltd.*[7] In its 2006 decision, the High Court of Australia confirmed by a 5-to-2 majority that it is not contrary to public policy for a funder to finance and control litigation in the expectation of profit, and that litigation funded on this basis does not amount to an abuse of the court's process.

In *Fostif*, the accounting company Firmstones funded a large number of class-action participants who were seeking reimbursement of license fees paid to tobacco wholesalers. Each individual claim was small and not cost-effective to bring on its own. Firm-stones essentially conceived, organized, and financed the entire class-action. They also indemnified all class-members against adverse cost orders by providing a substantial security guarantee, as losers pay the costs of the entire case in Australia.

Firmstones exercised a great deal of control over the litigation process. They hired the lawyers to act for the claimants and in-structed them not to interact with any of the claimants. They also issued all of the instructions to the lawyers in relation to the con-duct of the case. They had power to settle on behalf of the class, so long as the settlement was not less than 75 percent of the claim. For their efforts, Firmstones was to receive a third of all the pro-ceeds they collected from the defendants.

The High Court upheld the funding arrangement between Firmstones and class members. It pointed out that

> many people seek profit from assisting the processes of litiga-tion. That a person who hazards funds in litigation wishes to control the litigation is hardly surprising. That someone seeks out those who may have a claim and excites litigation where otherwise there would be none could be condemned as contrary to public policy only if a general rule against the maintenance of actions were to be adopted. But that approach has long since been abandoned.[8]

The *Fostif* decision heralded a resounding victory for advocates of third-party funding. It confirmed the legitimacy of the industry and clarified the level of control that can be exercised by funders.

The degree of control enjoyed by Firmstones over the litigation process, however, is uncommon even for Australia. Firmstones not only selected counsel for the plaintiffs but also controlled all communications with the class. Courts in other countries would likely view *Fostif* as a liberal interpretation of how legal finance should interact with the legal system. Allowing such control by a funding company would almost certainly outrage U.S. courts, which have yet to examine any recent cases where the funding company conceived and directed the litigation.

Nevertheless, the growth of the industry in Australia has not been without problems. The unregulated nature of litigation funding remains a live issue with critics who are continually concerned that consumers may be vulnerable to harm and abuse of court process. In 2009, the *Brookfield Multiplex* case injected a great deal of uncertainty for litigation funders in Australia, who faced the prospect of licensing before the Australian Securities and Investments Commission.[9] In that case, the Full Court of the Federal Court found that litigation funding arrangements constitute an unregistered managed investment scheme. Thereafter, the New South Wales Court of Appeal in *International Litigation Partners Pte. Ltd. v. Chameleon Mining Ltd.* also held that a funder of commercial litigation was required to be licensed by Australia's securities watchdog and that investments in lawsuits constituted credit facilities.[10]

However, the lively debate that ensued in the wake of these decisions produced a rapid reaction from lawmakers. In response to *Chameleon Mining*, Parliament enacted a change to the law, exempting litigation funding arrangements from securities registration so long as adequate procedures are followed for managing any conflict of interest that may arise in relation to the investment. The *Corporations Amendment Regulation 2012 (No. 6)* was made on 12 July 2012, clarifying that litigation funding schemes and similar arrangements were not managed investment schemes, and not subject to the regulatory requirements such as registration, licensing, and disclosure.[11] Moreover, the amendment expressly excludes litigation funding arrangements from being credit facilities.[12]

Perhaps the most striking feature of the new law is Parliament's endorsement of litigation funding on public policy grounds. In its explanatory statement to the amendment, the legislators stated:

This regulation promotes access to justice by providing an alternative mechanism for claimants to pursue their rights in court. This permits claims to be brought that might not otherwise have been brought in the absence of this reform. For example, the claimants may lack the financial resources to finance their lawsuit or where the compensation for individual claimants is likely to be too small to justify a lawsuit but where the compensation for the entire class is likely to be substantial.[13]

Despite repeated challenges to its model, few would suggest that Australia's burgeoning legal finance industry is not poised for continued growth. There are currently seven litigation funding companies in Australia. Two of these companies, IMF and Hillcrest Litigation Services Limited, are listed on the Australian Securities Exchange.

The Australian legal finance industry pioneered many methodologies now being applied by companies targeting markets in the United States and United Kingdom. It also provided very important metrics for evaluating risk in commercial deals. Perhaps most importantly, the development of the legal framework that enables legal finance in Australia serves as an important precedent for other jurisdictions, as the debate there shares many of the same features with those that are occurring in other countries. As the global industry matures, many continue to view Australia as the vanguard of the legal finance industry.

United Kingdom

The development of the legal finance market in the United Kingdom is interesting from a number of perspectives. Foremost, English law is often persuasive for courts and cited by jurists in other jurisdictions because it serves a foundation for all common-law countries, including the United States. Recent court cases in the United Kingdom, as well as reports by legal scholars, government agencies and professional organizations, have all confirmed the legality of legal finance transactions.

As in the United States, the United Kingdom has an enormous legal sector, generating more than £20 billion (roughly $32 billion) per year in revenue or nearly 2 percent of gross domestic product.[14] U.K. law firms are some of the largest in the world. Firms like Clifford Chance, Linklaters, Freshfields, and Allen & Overy consistently rank in the top 10 of the Global 100 top law firms. The United Kingdom is also a very international dispute resolution forum. Many international disputes are settled in U.K. courts and before arbitration bodies such as the London Court of International Arbitration and the London Maritime Arbitrators Association. For example, the majority of the world's maritime arbitration takes place in London.[15]

The United Kingdom also has very liquid and sophisticated capital markets, which like the United States are quick to adopt financial innovation. Companies that seek to explore this business model have enjoyed generous access to capital, as well as the availability of professional expertise necessary to institutionalize lawsuit investing. As most international law, accounting and finance firms have a large presence in London, there is greater opportunity for rapid transfer of new ideas to different markets. According to *Legal Week*, most of London's top law firms are already using or assessing external funding for litigation and arbitration cases.[16]

The debate about the proper role of legal finance (called litigation funding in the United Kingdom, as it is in Australia) unfurls as efforts to improve access to the legal system have gained greater importance. Like most other countries, the United Kingdom shifts costs of unsuccessful litigation to the losing party which is a safeguard intended to check the spread of frivolous lawsuits in society. It is also intended to indemnify litigants against legal costs they have unreasonably incurred as a matter of justice.

As previously mentioned, the English rule also has the undesirable effect of restricting access to justice, because many potential litigants are either unwilling to bring an action when faced with the prospect of paying for the defendant's costs or unable to afford the premiums associated with purchasing after-the-event insurance (available in many jurisdictions that follow the English Rule), which protects litigants from adverse results.

As modern legal systems seek to facilitate access, U.K. lawmakers increasingly view litigation funding as a critical tool to level the playing field. Like Australia, the United Kingdom has taken a liberal stance on third-party funding by relaxing the traditional limitations imposed by the champerty doctrine.

Champerty, as we have seen, traces its origin to the earliest periods of English history. It was the practice of wealthy men to buy up the often dubious claims of the poor in return for a share of the spoils as a means of settling scores against their rivals. To curtail this practice, public policy developed prohibiting champerty and maintenance, making them crimes in common law.

These doctrines, however, were never intended to deal with the realities of complex litigation in sophisticated legal systems. Rather, they were a reaction to the corruption and influence that powerful men exerted over the courts—abuses that became irrelevant with the advent of an independent judiciary. Recognizing a need to modernize English law, Parliament passed the Criminal Law Act of 1967, which abolished criminal and civil liability for champerty, along with several other obsolete offenses.[17]

Subsequent case law confirmed that public policy attitudes toward third-party funding in the United Kingdom had indeed changed. In *Hill v. Archbold*, a trade union had funded a libel action by two claimants of unlawful maintenance.[18] In that case, Lord Denning held that the trade union was not guilty of maintenance, arguing:

> Much maintenance is considered justifiable today which would in 1914 have been considered obnoxious. Most of the actions in our courts are supported by some association or other, or by

the state itself. Comparatively few litigants bring suits, or defend them, at their own expense. Most claims by workmen against their employers are paid for by a trade union. Most defences of motorists are paid for by insurance companies. This is perfectly justifiable and is accepted by everyone as lawful, provided always that the one who supports the litigation, if it fails, pays the costs of the other side.[19]

The climate for litigation funding in the United Kingdom became even more liberal when conditional fee agreements (CFAs), a form of contingent fees, were permitted in 1995. This had the effect of relaxing maintenance laws in personal injury claims, long a taboo outside the United States.

In the 2002 *Factortame* case,[20] the court was asked to examine an arrangement that had the potential of offending the traditional notions of champerty. In that case, the accounting firm Grant Thornton funded the lawsuit of Spanish fishermen in return for 8 percent of the recovery. Despite a champerty challenge, that arrangement was held to be lawful.

Subsequent decisions have continued to permit third-party funding. In the seminal 2005 case *Arkin v. Borchard Lines Ltd.*, the Court of Appeal confirmed that third-party funding was an acceptable means of financing lawsuits, so long as the funder does not control the management of the litigation.[21]

The plaintiff in *Arkin* was represented by his lawyers under a conditional fee arrangement. A third-party funder, MPC, also agreed to provide financial support to the claimant, paying for accounting experts and other related services in exchange for a percentage of the recovery. MPC estimated that their total cost of financing Mr. Arkin's claim was £1.3 million (about U.S. $2.4 million).

Under their agreement, the claimant was responsible for conducting the litigation, but needed the consent of MPC for any settlement agreement with the defendant. As the case progressed,

MPC made no attempt to control it. Even with MPC's participation, however, the defendant prevailed and the case was lost. Under the fee-shifting rule, Mr. Arkin was responsible for defendants' legal costs, which exceeded £6 million (about U.S. $11 million). The plaintiff could not pay and the defendant sought to recover all of it from MPC.

The Court of Appeal, the second most senior court, considered how third-party funders should be held liable for the costs of failed cases. It concluded:

> Somehow or other a just solution must be devised whereby on the one hand a successful opponent is not denied all his costs while on the other hand commercial funders who provide help to those seeking access to justice which they could not otherwise afford are not deterred by the fear of disproportionate costs consequences if the litigation they are supporting does not succeed.[22]

MPC was ultimately held liable for the defendant's costs on the basis of £1 in costs for every £1 invested.

In 2007, the Civil Justice Council, a Ministry of Justice–funded organization responsible for helping modernize civil justice in England and Wales, published a report in which it recommended litigation funding as an acceptable option. In that report, the council explained:

> The English courts have taken the view that third-party funding is now acceptable in the interests of access to justice, particularly where the prospective claimant is unable to fund their claim by any other means. In short, the individual's right to access to justice must ultimately be subsumed to the doctrinal concerns of champerty and maintenance.[23]

By 2008, the Law Society of England and Wales, the professional association that represents solicitors, also weighed in on the subject of third-party funding. In its report on litigation funding, the Society recognized that the industry will be a permanent fixture of the U.K. legal system. They explained: It can be said that third-party funding is well established and has been accepted by the courts as, in certain cases, a lawful means of funding litigation. It would not, therefore, seem appropriate for the Law Society to stand in the way of what is perceived to be another method of funding which increases access to justice.[24]

More recently, while making a number of proposals to reform civil justice and reduce costs in England and Wales, Sir Rupert Jackson, the distinguished judge of the Court of Appeal, confirmed that champerty and maintenance no longer apply in England and Wales. In his report *Review of Civil Litigation Costs: Final Report*,[25] he explained that courts in the United Kingdom and abroad now recognize that third-party funding facilitates access to justice for litigants. He concluded that it is preferable for plaintiffs to give up some their claim's value to a third party than to receive nothing.[26]

The acceptance of litigation funding in the United Kingdom, however, comes with a caveat. English courts have consistently held that champerty and maintenance prohibitions against third-party funding do not apply so long as investors do not control the plaintiffs or the underlying claims. Issues of control also trouble English courts because of the perceived interference with the attorney-client relationship that arises when a third party, rather than the claimant, is directing litigation. As a result, U.K. funding companies have sought to assure regulators that their investment practices are in line with public policy. In a typical funding transaction, the plaintiff decides which lawyers to hire. Furthermore, plaintiffs and their attorneys, not the investors, agree on case strategy and direct the prosecution of their claims. Moreover, the plaintiff will ultimately decide whether to settle the claim for a given amount.

Even if English courts are not as progressive as the Australian High Court regarding the degree of control the funder may have over the litigation process, the favorable legal climate has created the necessary impetus for the expansion of the industry. Fueled by a high demand for capital as a result of tight credit markets, litigation funding in the United Kingdom has gained momentum in recent years as some of the largest law firms began utilizing lawsuit-linked funding products.

While the climate for legal finance continues to improve in the United Kingdom, increased scrutiny of the industry has also produced calls for greater oversight. In his discussion of this industry, Sir Jackson recommended that a code be drawn up to which all third-party funders should subscribe. This code, according to the justice, should contain capital adequacy requirements and should restrict funders' ability to withdraw support for ongoing litigation.[27] In response to this call, a voluntary code of conduct, the Code of Conduct of Litigation Funders (the Code), has been drafted by the Civil Justice Council (CJC) in conjunction with the Association of Litigation Funders of England and Wales.[28] It became law in November 2011. The Code is a landmark development in legal finance because, for the first time, a law specifically recognizes the importance of third-party funding in litigation but also attempts to balance the right of lawsuit investors with their corresponding obligations to claimants and the justice system.

The Code requires lawsuit investors to give certain assurances to claimants regarding their participation in their claims. These assurances include, among other things, that the funder: (a) will not try to take over or control the litigation; (b) is adequately capitalized to fund the litigation; and (c) will not withdraw from funding a claim unless there is a material adverse development.[29]

In addition to confirming the previous limitations on exercising third-party control over litigation, the Code also attempts to mitigate some of the more recent abuses that have tarnished the industry. For example, the capital requirement is meant to dissuade parties form making unsubstantiated funding commitments. This is aimed at companies that misrepresent their ability to sustain the expenses of a lawsuit, whether because they are brokers without direct funding, or undercapitalized investors. The Code requires disclosure to litigants about funders' access to funds, requiring funders to have at a minimum sufficient capital to support their aggregate funding liabilities for at least 36 months.[30]

Similarly, the Code requires investors to specify the basis for terminating funding agreements with clients, allowing investors to withdraw only in the event of a material breach by clients or if the viability of the claim has substantially changed.[31] The Code, therefore, prohibits investors from unilaterally terminating funding commitments without some underlying material trigger.

Both of these requirements are central to the relationship between claimants and investors. Litigation is a very uncertain and long-term endeavor, requiring a significant commitment from both parties. Relying on funding sources that are undependable can be disastrous for any lawsuit. The Code recognizes this danger by providing greater transparency to claimants who are relying on third-party funding to sustain their disputes.

Over the past several years, commercial litigation funding in the United Kingdom has injected a great deal of momentum into the industry internationally, paving the way for a surge of institutional investment in this space. In addition to Juridica and Burford, both of which floated their shares on London's AIM, other U.K.-based legal finance providers include companies such as Harbour, Woodsford, Therium, and Calunius.

Conclusion

The great strides made in Australia and the United Kingdom toward acceptance of and mounting participation in legal financing speak both to the international market potential of the industry and the increasing likelihood that such progressive viewpoints may, over time, overtake more restrictive attitudes, including those found in many U.S. jurisdictions. The leadership Australia has demonstrated in the global legal finance market stands as a venerable example for the development of the industry in other countries. Likewise, the United Kingdom's position as a global financial and legal center has spurred the development of its own legal finance sector, and that growth, in turn, has given rise organically to efforts at voluntary self-regulation. The development of legal finance in Australia and the United Kingdom alike demonstrate natural courses of evolution for the industry of which other countries—the United States among them—should take notice.

CHAPTER 8

THE FUTURE OF LEGAL FINANCE

As preceding chapters have shown, the need for legal finance arose organically from the unequal access to justice endemic to many modern legal systems—the United States notable among them. Companies like Plaintiff Support Services and Future Settlement Funding pioneered the industry in the 1990s, at a time when most U.S. courts had already begun to view the doctrines of champerty, maintenance, and barratry as obsolete. The industry quickly expanded to offer three main product lines: lawsuit advances for tort claims, funding for commercial matters, and loan products tailored to help attorneys and law firms finance case costs and overhead expenses.

In the United States, tort and commercial litigation comprise most of the millions of civil cases filed each year. Moreover, nearly 40 percent of all tort matters and a similar percentage of commercial claims are never filed in court, and many others are resolved through alternative dispute resolution methods like arbitration. There is understandably great financial momentum in the U.S. legal system. Nevertheless, due to a dearth of resources often required to participate in that system, a sizable portion of aggrieved parties never attain the redress they deserve.

Legal finance products help bridge this gap. Lawsuit advances for tort plaintiffs give injured parties the ability to pay for living expenses that they cannot handle alone. Financing for commercial plaintiffs provides similar relief and support for businesses that could otherwise face insolvency while devoting so many of their resources towards litigation. Meanwhile, legal finance for intellectual property has developed into a multi-billion-dollar industry over the course of more than thirty years, and specifically tailored financing—in the form of contingent advances, lines of credit, case expense loans, post-settlement funding or fee acceleration— can enable law firms themselves to pursue and conclude claims that otherwise would fall beyond the scope of their wherewithal.

The process of lawsuit investing itself is, by necessity, complex. The origination of investment opportunities alone involves the use of multiple marketing channels to originate deals, attorney referrals, and brokers. Underwriting is a critical step in the investment process, ensuring that funders receive the return they expect, and that a myriad of potential problems are avoided. The challenge then posed in structuring effective funding agreements lies in striking a balance between the enforceability and flexibility of the document while keeping its terms attractive to clients and attorneys. Funders and their compliance teams must exercise vigilance in managing their investments for the entire life of the claim. Yet the most important factor running through all phases of the investment process is a funder's relationships with the attorneys and law firms driving the legal claims. Respecting the attorney's role, the obligations of the attorney-client relationship, and especially the attorney him or herself—through courtesy, clear communication, and understanding—solidifies the working partnership among funder, attorney, and client that underlies the investment process.

Despite its immense potential to help disadvantaged claimants, law firms, and interested investors alike, legal finance is not without controversy. Yet detractors generally resort to blanket criticisms that do not distinguish between the various products offered by the industry. Other critics erect straw-man caricatures that unfairly distort the legal finance process in ways that lend themselves to easy disparagement. And many other would-be doomsayers often portend slippery-slope consequences for the litigation system that inevitably fail to materialize. When examined in context, without hyperbole and in concert with statistical data collected on the industry, the most bombastic concerns about legal finance fall to the wayside.

The general trend is toward wider acceptance of legal finance in most states. Notwithstanding, a fair amount of uncertainty lingers with regard to how courts in several jurisdictions would interpret legal finance deals. In fact, the current state of the law and its application is very disparate. Whether a jurisdiction continues to recognize restrictions on maintenance and champerty can affect the enforceability of legal finance agreements, with most states permitting some forms while maintaining prohibitions of varying degrees. Contractual considerations like unconscionability and the validity of mandatory arbitration clauses, assignments, state regulatory efforts, and even regulations pertaining to the conduct of attorneys all play a role in determining whether a legal finance agreement can—or will—be upheld in court.

The legal finance industries of Australia and the United Kingdom compare and contrast with their U.S. counterpart in several illuminating ways. While they all share a common lineage in the English common law tradition, the respective legal finance industries in Australia and the United Kingdom provide useful examples worth considering when contemplating the further development of legal finance in the United States. Progressive high court decisions in Australia have spurred tremendous growth of the industry, which in turn yielded both a proliferation of opportunities and potential pitfalls. Australian legal finance leaders continue to vanguard the industry, pioneering many methodologies that are now being applied in the United States and United Kingdom alike. Likewise the enormity of the United Kingdom's legal sector, the internationality of its dispute resolution forum, and the centrality of its capital markets on the world stage have cultivated a climate favorable to legal finance, despite the less progressive leanings of U.K. courts. The development of legal finance in both countries demonstrates natural courses of evolution for the industry of which other countries—including the United States—should take notice.

The coming years dawn cautiously bright for the legal finance industry. Despite some regulatory resistance and lingering stigma, legal finance is poised to continue its ascent in the United States and internationally. What started out as a cottage industry in the mid-nineties has acquired considerable momentum over the past several years, particularly in emerging niches like commercial funding and lending to law firms. As third-party funding matures and business models are tested across different markets, many expect legal finance to become a permanent feature of the global legal sector.

A number of factors contribute to this trend.

Foremost, information about new products now spreads at unprecedented rates, creating a deeper understanding of legal finance among a much broader range of participants. The communications revolution has made more accurate information about this field increasingly available to the public, helping dispel some of the myths that have previously contributed to stigmatizing the industry, while bolstering its credibility through greater market knowledge. The past several years have witnessed a proliferation of poignant scholarly debate, as a number of law review articles, research reports, and studies have examined many of the central issues relating to this field. The media has also contributed to the discourse, as an increasing number of articles in newspapers such as the *New York Times*, the *Wall Street Journal*, magazines, and trade journals have piqued the public's interest. The Internet has further enabled market participants to disseminate information about their industry through a growing number of providers' websites, blogs, videos and seminars, as well as the appearance of online trade publications like the *Legal Finance Journal*. Industry presentations and conferences have recently grown in popularity, allowing the industry engage with their colleagues, investors and legal professionals on a more personal level.

In addition, the laws, regulations and legal precedent relating to third-party funding are becoming more developed in the United States as an increasing number of states examine legal finance transactions. Largely through the efforts of ALFA, a template for regulating the industry is beginning to emerge, as several states have passed a regulatory framework for legal finance, many elements of which are being considered by other states as well as influential organizations, such as the National Conference of Insurance Legislators (NCOIL) and the American Bar Association, for inclusion into their model legislation. Institutional acceptance of legal finance in jurisdictions like Australia and the United Kingdom has also created important validation for the industry, demonstrating its efficacy and compatibility with modern legal systems.

Systemic economic changes are contributing to the expansion of legal finance. The cash crunch and widespread austerity measures continue to drive demand for monetizing lawsuit assets. The 2008 financial crisis significantly eroded personal wealth, while also impacting businesses of all sizes, making them less capable of financing the costs of protracted litigation. Municipalities, schools, and non-profit organizations have also experienced liquidity constraints, which have similarly impeded their access to justice.

All of this has occurred against a backdrop of escalating legal costs, which are exacerbated by lengthy discovery and clogged judicial dockets that continue to extend disposition times. Over the past several years, accident victims have increasingly relied on tort funding companies to pay for medical treatment that is not covered by the victims' or defendants' insurance. Housing is another area where individuals have needed help. By some estimates, nearly 60 percent of all tort advances are now used to pay for housing and frequently to avoid foreclosure. Commercial funders have too seen an expansion of their respective market.

Juridica, for example, has funded Fortune 1000 companies, FT Global 500 companies, as well as inventors, major universities, and the leading law firms that represent them.[1]

The legal industry has also been affected by the global financial crisis, precipitating a more rapid modernization of the sector, which is becoming more receptive to legal finance products. An increasing number of law firms have looked to legal finance firms for the capital needs. For example, lawsuit lender Counsel Financial has funded hundreds of contingency law firms and Burford has also participated in deals with law firms, including AmLaw 100 firms representing large companies.[2] In one case, Burford has helped Simpson Thatcher prevail in high stakes litigation against an Arizona real estate developer, which resulted in $110 million verdict.[3]

According to a recent survey, more than 90 percent of commercial litigators and corporate general counsels are aware of legal finance and most expect the industry to grow in the coming years.[4] In addition, the majority of litigators also indicated having a case that would have benefited from legal finance products; however, only a small minority have ever used them.[5] The more pervasive use of legal finance providers by top law firms will inexorably become a catalyst for much wider adoption of these products by the legal industry.

Moreover, institutional investors are increasingly backing the expansion of legal finance. For years, institutions have been relegated to interacting with the legal system as litigants rather than investors. They have seen firsthand the enormous scale of the legal sector, but have never had a meaningful opportunity to participate in any other capacity. A greater number of investors, however, are beginning to understand the potential of this field and are contributing more capital to fund an increasing number of legal assets.

For investors, legal finance offers an attractive value proposition: scalability and substantial absolute returns, which are uncorrelated to traditional assets like equities, fixed income, foreign exchange, and commodities.

In particular, lawsuit-linked products targeting businesses and law firms offer significant scalability to investors. Since its formation, Counsel Financial has loaned more than $600 million to law firms. Juridica has invested approximately $157 million in 23 cases across 18 investments.[6] Burford has committed more than $332 million in 43 investments since inception,[7] while Australia's IMF has invested in 162 cases, generating more than AU $1.2 billion (about U.S. $1.25 billion) in revenue.[8] The company currently has a portfolio consisting of 25 cases, with a total claim value amounting to approximately AU $1.2 billion (about U.S. $1.25 billion).[9] With scale comes significant opportunities for securitization, allowing larger investors to add lawsuit assets to their investment portfolios. For some investors, like insurance companies, lawsuit-linked products may be a natural hedge. Large insurers such as Axa, Fidelity, and Prudential have already made sizeable investments in this space.[10]

Legal finance offers an opportunity for portfolio diversification and long term wealth appreciation. The performance data for legal finance companies is compelling. For example, Juridica has posted a gross internal rate of return from the seven investments which have reached completion of approximately 85 percent through June 2012[11] and Burford announced in 2012 a 70 percent return on proceeds from its first 14 settled cases.[12] Similarly, IMF has demonstrated stellar performance in over a decade of investing in lawsuits. A public company in Australia, IMF has concluded 137 claims, of which 93 resulted in settlements, 12 were won at trial, 27 were withdrawn, and 5 were lost.[13] The average investment period for IMF's cases is 2.3 years, with an average gross return of 310 percent during this period.[14] In 2012, IMF has increased its net income by 86 percent from AU $38 million (about U.S. $40 million) to AU $70.5 million (about U.S. $73 million).[15]

At the same time, analysis of IMF's settlement data points to a correlation to the benchmark S&P/ASX 200 index of just 0.01.[16] If claims are spread out over different law firms and jurisdictions, investments are also generally uncorrelated to each other. Furthermore, the strategy is largely countercyclical to the larger economy: during economic contractions there is generally more litigation but less money to pay for it.

As performance metrics from resolved cases become increasingly available, more and more investors are taking a closer look at opportunities available in legal finance. Several developments are certain to emerge as the industry expands. Inevitably, new products will address a broader range of legal markets, while also making capital available to more types of cases within those specialties. In the consumer market, providers will continue to increase their participation in funding medical procedures, by forging relationships with medical providers, who are becoming important referral sources for the industry. Similarly, divorce funding is become a new frontier for lawsuit investors, as several new entrants are actively raising capital to deploy in this space. One new entrant, Balance Point Divorce Funding, has recently raised $15 million to deploy in divorce claims.[17] Similarly, inheritance advances offer a compelling value proposition to beneficiaries and a familiar business model to funding companies. Companies such as Heir Advance already provide immediate funding to heirs against their expected probate proceeds.

In the commercial market, providers are becoming more international in their reach, expanding their business models to Hong Kong, Singapore, and even a number of European countries with civil law legal systems. They also support a growing number of arbitration proceedings. The financing of class actions is also likely to benefit from legal finance as some of the larger funding companies expand their activities into this space, a practice that has been successfully implemented by IMF in Australia.

In addition to legal finance products designed for plaintiffs and law firms, investors with large balance sheets are also likely to offer a new class of products specifically created for defendants, which will function more like after-the-event insurance by shifting some of the litigation risk to a repeat player: the funding company. Imagine for a moment that a corporate defendant is involved in high-stakes litigation, which it estimates will cost $100 million or more in costs and damages if it loses. The defendant may strike an agreement with a legal finance provider to fund the defense of the claim in exchange for a portion of the damages saved (e.g., a verdict or settlement that falls below $100 million). Such an arrangement can have the effect of not only protecting against litigation costs, but also mitigating the downside arising from adverse decisions.

As competition continues to grow, legal finance companies will become more integrated in the future, offering a number of different products to plaintiffs, defendants and the legal industry. Companies such as LawCash and Burford are leading this trend. LawCash has offered consumer tort advances to plaintiffs since 2001, but has now branched out into providing banking services to attorneys through its affiliate, Esquire Bank. The bank offers a number of novel products for attorneys, including case cost financing, fee acceleration, a legal practice management suite, as well as settlement debit cards for plaintiffs that are co-branded with law firms.[18] Burford has recently acquired U.K. after-the-event insurance provider Firstassist Legal Expenses, gaining a sales platform for lawsuit-linked insurance products and relationships with hundreds of law firms.[19] As providers focus on revenue growth, more combinations are certain to follow as companies expand their collaboration with niche players and take advantage of complimentary business models.

The pace of information exchange will continue to accelerate. As more performance data becomes available, providers will continue to fine tune their business models, growing increasingly sophisticated through iterative improvements to their investment processes and underwriting methodologies. They will become more technologically savvy by implementing new systems to mitigate risk and increase productivity.

The regulation of legal finance will also converge across different jurisdictions, primarily as a consequence of globalization in the legal sector. Many of the issues that funders contend with in their jurisdictions, whether foreign or domestic, are also relevant in other places, and lawmakers will increasingly look to other markets for effective ways of dealing with issues relating to legal finance. This is already evident in the ongoing debate over how much control investors should exercise over the litigation process. This convergence, however, will not always benefit providers. One danger is that adverse case law and onerous regulatory require-ments may be imported from other jurisdictions. For example, as legal systems look for ways to deal with escalating legal costs and special interests continue to lobby for tort reform, investors may become increasingly subject to the expansive use of fee shifting laws, which can hold them accountable for paying defense costs in unsuccessful claims. This is already a significant risk for funders in the United Kingdom, and at least one U.S. court has already examined this issue to a funder's detriment.

"Slings and Arrows of outrageous Fortune" continue to afflict people today much as they did in Shakespeare's time. That is unlikely to change. What has and will continue to change is the degree of financial support available to the afflicted when their fate depends on a costly legal system. Those who suffer a serious car accident like Tim and Caroline will not have to make do with a pennies-on-the-dollar insurance settlement; they can acquire the funds they need to meet their day-to-day expenses long enough to achieve the justice their case deserves. In-house counsel like Susan will be able to pursue worthwhile lawsuits without risking her company's future. Inventors like Jonathan will be able to defend his patented inventions from misappropriation. Attorneys like Anne and David will be able to properly champion disabled children in their state without imperiling the solvency of their law firm or the livelihoods of its employees. All of them—and countless others with strong legal cases but inadequate financial means to pursue them—will be poised to attain justice in their lives because of the opportunities and resources that only legal finance can offer.

NOTES

Chapter 1

1 Robert Moskowitz, *Access to Justice, Access to Funds*, LEGAL FIN. J. (Apr. 1, 2011), http://legalfinancejournal.com/access-to-justice-access-to-funds/.

2 Stewart Levine, *The Many Costs of Conflict*, LAW PRACTICE TODAY (Dec. 2006), http://apps.americanbar.org/lpm/lpt/articles/mba12061.shtml.

3 John Henry, *Fortune 500: The Total Cost of Litigation Estimated at One-Third Profits*, THE METROPOLITAN CORPORATE COUNSEL (Feb. 2008), http://www.metrocorpcounsel.com/pdf/2008/February/28.pdf.

4 LAWYERS FOR CIVIL JUSTICE, CIVIL JUSTICE REFORM GROUP & U.S. CHAMBER INSTITUTE FOR LEGAL REFORM, LITIGATION COST SURVEY OF MAJOR COMPANIES 2 (2010), *available at* http://www.uscourts.gov/uscourts/RulesAndPolicies/rules/Duke%20Materials/Library/Litigation%20Cost%20Survey%20of%20Major%20Companies.pdf.

5 *Id.* at 2.

6 *Id.* at 3.

7 *Compare* PRICE WATERHOUSE COOPERS, 2011 PATENT LITIGATION STUDY: PATENT LITIGATION TRENDS AS THE "AMERICA INVENTS ACT" BECOMES LAW 8 (2011), *available at* http://www.pwc.com/us/en/forensic-services/publications/assets/2011-patent-litigation-study.pdf, *with* JAMES C. PISTORINO & SUSAN J. CRANE, 2011 TRENDS IN PATENT CASE FILINGS: EASTERN DISTRICT OF TEXAS CONTINUES TO LEAD UNTIL AMERICA INVENTS ACT IS SIGNED 1 (2011), *available at* http://www.perkinscoie.com/files/upload/PL_12_03PistorinoArticle.pdf.

8 AMERICAN INTELLECTUAL PROPERTY LAW ASSOCIATION (AIPLA), REPORT OF THE ECONOMIC SURVEY 2011, At I-153–154.

9 LAWYERS FOR CIVIL JUSTICE, *supra* note 4, at 3.

10 *Id.*

11 *Id.*

12 *Id.*

13 THE WORLD JUSTICE PROJECT, RULE OF LAW INDEX, 2012 161 (2012). *See also* Anthony Sebok, *Helping Ordinary People*, N.Y. TIMES, Nov. 16, 2010, *available at* http://www.nytimes.com/roomfordebate/2010/11/15/investing-in-someone-elses-lawsuit/helping-ordinary-people.

14 See Earl Johnson, Jr., *Equal Access to Justice: Comparing Access to Justice in the United States and Other Industrial Democracies*, 24 FORDHAM INT'L L.J. 83 (2001) (discussing the inadequate level of funds provided for legal services in the United States in comparison with other countries).

15 THE WORLD JUSTICE PROJECT, *supra* note 13, at 27.

16 Gillian Hadfield, *Lawyers, Make room For Nonlawyers*, at http://www.cnn.com/2012/11/23/opinion/hadfield-legal-profession/index.html.

17 M. Craig Tyler, *Patent Pirates Search for Texas Treasure*, TEX. LAWYER (Sept. 20, 2004), *available at* http://www.wsgr.com/PDFSearch/09202004_patentpirates.pdf.

18 *In re K.A.H.*, 967 P.2d 91, 93 (Alaska 1998) (noting that "defendants, aware of the economic pressure burdening unaided plaintiffs, have every economic incentive to prolong the litigation with frivolous motions and discovery").

19 Jonathan T. Molot, *Litigation Finance: A Market Solution to a Procedural Problem*, 99 GEO. L.J. 65, 83–84 (2010).

20 *Id.* at 83–84.

21 35 U.S.C. § 261 of the U.S. Patent Act specifically authorizes transfers of patents. The majority of the world's patent infringement lawsuits occur in the United States.

22 *See, e.g,* Aaron Smith, *Merck Stock Tumbles After Vioxx Verdict*, CNN MONEY (Apr. 6, 2006, 5:45 PM), http://money.cnn.com/2006/04/06/news/companies/merck_outlook/index.htm. *See also* Jonathan Stempel & Alistair Sharp, *BlackBerry Maker RIM Sued by NXP Over Patents*, REUTERS (Apr. 3, 2012, 3:31 PM), http://www.reuters.com/article/2012/04/03/us-researchinmotion-nxp-idUSBRE8320O120120403.

23 *See, e.g.*, Clare Jim, *HTC Shares Tumble as Patent Case Delays U.S. Sales*, REUTERS (May 16, 2012, 2:55 AM), http://www.reuters.com/article/2012/05/16/us-htc-idUS-BRE84F05L20120516. *See also* Alexander Eichler, *Bank of America Stock Falls 20 Percent After $10 Billion Lawsuit*, HUFFINGTON POST, Aug. 8, 2011, *available at* http://www.huffingtonpost.com/2011/08/08/bofa-stock_n_921648.html.

24 Susan Lorde Martin, *Syndicated Lawsuits: Illegal Champerty or New Business Opportunity?*, 30 AM. BUS. L.J. 485, 492 (1992).

25 Yifat Shaltiel & John Cofresi, *Litigation Lending for Personal Needs Act: A Regulatory Framework to Legitimize Litigation Finance*, 58 CONSUMER FIN. L.Q. REP. 347 (2004).

26 Edmund Andrews, *Patents; Financing Inventors' Lawsuits*, N.Y. TIMES, Mar. 11, 1989, at http://www.nytimes.com/1989/03/11/business/patents-financing-inventors-lawsuits.html. *See also Surf's Up, Patent-Wise, for Charles Hall, Father of the*

Modern Water Bed, PEOPLE MAGAZINE, May 6, 1991, Vol. 35, No. 17, *available at* http://www.people.com/people/archive/article/0,,20115047,00.html.

27 Poonam Puri, *Financing of Litigation by Third-Party Investors: A Share of Justice?*, 36 OSGOODE HALL L.J. 540, 541 (1998). *See also* Paul Sweeney, *Investing; How to Win Big in Court and Never See a Lawyer*, N.Y. TIMES, Nov. 1, 1998, *available at* http://www.nytimes.com/1998/11/01/business/investing-how-to-win-big-in-court-and-never-see-a-lawyer.html. For a good discussion on the savings and loan litigation, see United States v. Winstar Corp., 518 U.S. 839 (1996).

28 Osprey, Inc., v. Cabana, 340 S.C. 367, 375, 532 S.E.2d 269, 277 (S.C. 2008) (citing the seminal article on the subject: Max Radin, *Maintenance by Champerty*, 24 CAL. L. REV. 48, 58–64 (1935)).

29 Julia H. McLaughlin, *Litigation Funding: Charting a Legal and Ethical Course*, 31 VT. L. REV. 615, 639. *See also* Susan Lorde *Martin, Financing Plaintiffs' Lawsuits: An Increasingly Popular (and Legal) Business*, 33 MICH. J.L. REF. 57, 58 (1999).

30 *See generally* Peter Karsten, *Enabling the Poor to Have Their Day in Court: The Sanctioning of Contingency Fee Contracts, A History to 1940*, 47 DEPAUL L. REV. 231 (1998).

31 *Id.* at 236.

32 *Id.* at 236–237.

33 Key v. Vattier, 1 Ohio 132, 146 (1823).

34 Karsten, *supra* note 30, at 236.

35 *Id.*

36 Susan Lorde Martin, *Financing Litigation On-Line: Usury and Other Obstacles*, De Paul Bus. & Com. L.J., Vol. 1, No. 1, Fall 2002, 85, 86.

37 Several years later, after retiring from practicing law, DiNardo acquired Plaintiff Support Services from Polowitz.

38 Saladini v. Righellis, 426 Mass. 231, 687 N.E.2d 1224 (1997).

Chapter 2

1 This number is the author's estimate and assumes the sum of all hourly legal fees collected by law firms, all fees collected by legal services firms, and the aggregate amounts paid to settle tort and commercial claims.

2 NATIONAL CENTER FOR STATE COURTS, COURT STATISTICS PROJECT, EXAMINING THE WORK OF STATE COURTS: AN ANALYSIS OF 2010 STATE COURT CASELOADS 8 (2011).

3 ADMINISTRATIVE OFFICE OF THE UNITED STATES COURTS. 2011 ANNUAL REPORT OF THE DIRECTOR: JUDICIAL BUSINESS OF THE UNITED STATES COURTS 10 (2012).

4 NATIONAL SAFETY COUNCIL, INJURY FACTS 4 (2011).

5 *See generally* U.S. DEPARTMENT OF TRANSPORTATION, TRAFFIC SAFETY FACTS 2010: A

COMPILATION OF MOTOR VEHICLE CRASH DATA FROM THE FATALITY ANALYSIS REPORTING SYSTEM AND THE GENERAL ESTIMATES SYSTEM (2011).

6 BUREAU OF LABOR STATISTICS, NEWS RELEASE: WORKPLACE INJURIES AND ILLNESSES—2011 (OCT. 25, 2012), *available at* http://www.bls.gov/news.release/osh.nr0.htm.

7 NATIONAL FLOOR SAFETY INSTITUTE, *available at* http://www.nfsi.org/the_costs.php.

8 NATIONAL SAFETY COUNCIL, *supra* note 4, at 2.

9 NATIONAL CENTER FOR STATE COURTS, *supra* note 2, at 11 (showing that approximately 6 percent of all incoming civil cases in 17 general jurisdiction courts in 2010 were tort related). *See also* BUREAU OF JUSTICE STATISTICS, FEDERAL TORT TRIALS AND VERDICTS, 2002-03 1 (2005).

10 NATIONAL CENTER FOR STATE COURTS, COURT STATISTICS PROJECT, EXAMINING THE WORK OF STATE COURTS: AN ANALYSIS OF 2008 STATE COURT CASELOADS 27 (2009) (showing that tort cases fell by 25 percent from 1999-2008 in 13 general jurisdiction courts).

11 BUREAU OF JUSTICE STATISTICS, CIVIL BENCH AND JURY TRIALS IN STATE COURTS, 2005 10 (2008).

12 *Id.* at 9.

13 *Id.* at 4.

14 *Id.* at 8.

15 *Id.* at 5.

16 VERDICTSEARCH, TOP 100 VERDICTS OF 2011, *available at* http://www.verdictsearch.com/index.jsp?do=top100.

17 NATIONAL CENTER FOR STATE COURTS, *supra* note 10.

18 NATIONAL CENTER FOR STATE COURTS, *supra* note 2, at 11 (showing that approximately 61 percent of all incoming civil cases in 17 general jurisdiction courts in 2010 were contract related).

19 BUREAU OF JUSTICE STATISTICS, *supra* note 11, at 4.

20 *Id.*

21 *Id.* at 8.

22 *Id.* at 5.

23 VERDICTSEARCH, *supra* note 16.

24 Gauer Distinguished Lecture in Law and Public Policy, Sponsored by the National Legal Center for the Public Interest, Stephen Breyer, Associate Justice, Supreme Court of the United States, *The Legal Profession and Public Service*, The Pierre Hotel, New York, NY, Sept. 12, 2000 (quoting Douglas W. Hillman, *Professionalism—A Plea for Action!*, 69 MICH. BAR J. 894, 895 (1990)).

25 Danny Yadron, *112th Congress: By the Numbers*, WALL STREET JOURNAL BLOGS: WASHINGTON WIRE, Jan. 5, 2011, http://blogs.wsj.com/washwire/2011/01/05/112th-congress-by-the-numbers/.

26 Dan Slater, *Barack Obama: The U.S.'s 44th President (and 25th Lawyer-President!)*, WALL STREET JOURNAL BLOGS: LAW BLOG, Nov. 5, 2008, http://blogs.wsj.com/law/2008/11/05/barack-obama-the-uss-44th-president-and-24th-lawyer-president/.

27 FIRST RESEARCH, LEGAL SERVICES, *available at* http://www.marketresearch.com/partners/811788012/First-Research-Inc-v3470/Legal-Services-7143411/.

28 Two contracting parties are free to select any arbitrator in almost any forum. For example, a buyer and seller may agree to use their trade organization to administer binding arbitration.

29 Convention of June 10, 1958, 21 U.S.T. 2517, T.I.A.S. No. 6997, 330 U.N.T.S. 38.

30 *Id.*

31 Mark Bezant, James Nicholson & Howard Rosen, *Dispute Resolution in the New Economy*, FTI JOURNAL, Apr. 2010, *available at*: http://www.ftijournal.com/article/Dispute-Resolution-in-the-Global-Economy.

32 BUREAU OF JUSTICE STATISTICS, CIVIL JURY CASES AND VERDICTS IN LARGE COUNTIES 1 (1995).

Chapter 3

1 ABA Rules of Professional Conduct Rule 1.8(e) prohibits a lawyer from lending money to a client with the exception of advancing court costs and expenses of litigation.

2 As custodians, attorneys typically maintain specialized bank accounts for purposes of receiving, holding and disbursing their clients' and third-parties' funds to facilitate certain transactions or settlements.

3 Binyamin Appelbaum, *Lobby Battle Over Loans for Lawsuits*, N.Y. TIMES, March 9, 2011, *available at* http://www.nytimes.com/2011/03/10/business/10lawsuits.html?_r=1&ref=binyaminappelbaum.

4 BOARD OF GOVERNORS OF THE FEDERAL RESERVE, CONSUMER CREDIT, *available at*: http://www.federalreserve.gov/releases/g19/current/.

5 Matthew Zeitlin, *JP Morgan, Wells Fargo, and Homeowners Profit with Help from the Fed*, THE DAILY BEAST, Oct. 12, 2012, http://www.thedailybeast.com/articles/2012/10/12/jpmorgan-wells-fargo-and-homeowners-profit-with-help-from-the-fed.html.

6 A current list of ALFA members can be found at http://www.americanlegalfin.com/OfficersAndMembers.asp.

7 During their underwriting review, funding companies will usually consider only the compensatory damages relating to a claim and will ignore any consequential or punitive damages.

8 In some cases, attorneys will provide representation on a contingency basis and may pay for all litigation expenses. In these situations, plaintiffs will seek to raise money for either personal expenses or working capital.

9 *See infra* Chapter 4 for a more detailed discussion of legal finance structuring.

10 It is not yet clear whether U.S. courts will uphold arrangements where third parties have any degree of control over the settlement process. It is likely that U.S courts, at least in the short term, will follow the U.K. convention and will be similarly reluctant to allow funders to direct settlement outcomes.

11 Bentham Capital is the U.S. arm of the Australian litigation funding company, IMF.

12 Fulbrook Management was established in 2011 by Selvyn Siedel, one of the founders of Burford.

13 Companies like Lighthouse and U.S. Claims invest primarily in tort cases, but also fund smaller commercial claims.

14 35 U.S.C. § 261 of the U.S. Patent Act specifically authorizes transfers of patents. The majority of the world's patent infringement lawsuits occur in the United States.

15 Lord Daniel Brennan, QC, *Third Party Litigation Funding and Claim Transfer, A Common Perspective From Common Law*, in GEOFFREY MCGOVERN ET AL., THIRD-PARTY LITIGATION FUNDING AND CLAIM TRANSFER: TRENDS AND IMPLICATIONS FOR THE CIVIL JUSTICE SYSTEM 49, 51 (UCLA-RAND CTR. L. & POL'Y 2010), *available at* http://www.rand.org/pubs/conf_proceedings/2010/RAND_CF272.pdf.

16 Robert W. Welkos, *Digging for the Truth*, LOS ANGELES TIMES, March 12, 2000, available at http://articles.latimes.com/2000/mar/12/entertainment/ca-7856/4.

17 MICHAEL J. SWANSON, HOW DAVID BEATS GOLIATH, ACCESS TO CAPITAL FOR CONTINGENT-FEE LAW FIRMS 56 (2011).

18 *Id.* at 85.

19 *Id.* at 89.

20 Binyamin Appelbaum, *Investors Put Money on Lawsuits to Get Payouts*, N.Y. TIMES, NOV. 14, 2010, *available at*: http://www.nytimes.com/2010/11/15/business/15lawsuit.html?_r=0.

21 Interview with Joseph Dinardo, Director and Founder, Counsel Financial (Aug. 1, 2012).

22 *Id.*

23 Appelbaum, *supra* note 20.

Chapter 4

1 Interview with Joseph DiNardo, Director and Founder, Counsel Financial (Aug. 1, 2012).

2 *Id.* However, this is being blurred by the fact that commercial funding providers like Juridica and Burford increasingly structure their deals as loans to law firms.

3 *See generally* DEPARTMENT OF LEGISLATIVE SERVICES, NEGLIGENCE SYSTEMS: CONTRIBU-TORY NEGLIGENCE, COMPARATIVE FAULT, AND JOINT AND SEVERAL LIABILITY (2004).

4 Attorneys' contingency fees typically increase if cases go to trial. Fees may also increase if a verdict is appealed by the defendant.

5 Perfected liens are liens for which the owner has established a priority right in the encumbered property with respect to other third parties. Perfection is typically accomplished by taking certain steps required by law to give third parties notice of the lien, such as filing a statement under the Uniform Commercial Code (UCC) for example.

6 If an attorney releases proceeds that rightfully belong to Medicare, the attorney will most likely be liable for that money.

7 Some U.S.-based tort advance companies also fund Canadian cases. Several commercial funders invest in Canadian, European and even Asian claims.

8 Violet Marmor, *Risky Business: The Dangers of Undervaluing Compliance*, LEGAL FIN. J. (MAY 16, 2011), http://legalfinancejournal.com/risky-business-the-dangers-of-undervaluing-compliance/.

9 *Id.*

Chapter 5

1 NATIONAL CENTER FOR STATE COURTS, COURT STATISTICS PROJECT, EXAMINING THE WORK OF STATE COURTS: AN ANALYSIS OF 2008 STATE COURT CASELOADS 27 (2009) (showing that tort cases fell by 25 percent from 1999-2008 in 13 general jurisdiction courts).

2 Bates. v. State Bar of Arizona, 433 U.S. 350, 376 (1977).

3 JOHN BEISNER, JESSICA MILLER & GARY RUBIN, U.S. CHAMBER INST. FOR LEGAL REFORM, SELLING LAWSUITS, BUYING TROUBLE: THIRD-PARTY LITIGATION FUNDING IN THE UNITED STATES (2009).

4 *Id.* at 5-6.

5 LORD JUSTICE JACKSON, REVIEW OF CIVIL LITIGATION COSTS, FINAL REPORT, MINISTRY OF JUSTICE 117 (2009) (ENG.).

6 *Available at* http://americanlegalfin.com/IndustryBestPractices.asp.

7 A copy of the agreement is available at http://www.americanlegalfin.com/alfasite2/documents/ ALFAAgreementWithAttorneyGeneral.pdf.

8 Consumer Legal Funding: An Overview of Best Practices and Financing Models, Presented by Amy M. Au, Esq., President, Alliance for Responsible Consumer Legal Funding, presentation Litigation Finance and Investment Summit, New York, NY, Apr. 27-29.

9 Leader Technologies, Inc. v. Facebook, Inc., 2010 WL 2545960 (D. Del. June 24, 2010).

10 Mondis Technology, Ltd., v. LG Electronics, Inc., 2011 WL 1714304 (E.D. Tex.).

11 Devon IT, Inc., v. IBM Corp, 2012 WL 4748160 (E.D. Pa.).

Chapter 6

1 Johnson v. Wright, 682 N.W.2d 671 (Minn. App. 2004).

2 Rancman v. Interim Settlement Funding Corp., 99 Ohio St.3d 121, 2003-Ohio-2721.

3 Maine and Ohio have passed legislation that directly regulates legal finance transactions in those states. Maine requires legal finance companies to register with the state and to include specific provisions in their funding agreements. Ohio enacted a similar law, thereby overruling a 2003 Ohio Supreme Court decision, *Rancman v. Interim Settlement Funding Corp*, which voided a legal finance agreement on the basis of maintenance and champerty.

4 Anthony J. Sebok, *The Inauthentic Claim*, 64 VAND. L. REV. 61 (2011).

5 *Id*. at 99 n.162.

6 *Id*. at 107 n.190.

7 Saladini v. Righellis, 426 Mass. 231, 687 N.E.2d 1224, 1226 (1997).

8 Kraft v. Mason, 668 So. 2d 679 (Fla. App. 4th Dist. 1996).

9 Osprey, Inc. v. Cabana Ltd. Partnership, 340 S.C. 367, 532 S.E.2d 269, 277 (2000).

10 *Id*. at 277.

11 Bluebird Partners v. First Fid. Bank, 94 N.Y.2d 726, 736 (2000).

12 *Id*.

13 Grossman v. Schlosser, 244 N.Y.S.2d 749, 750-751 (App. Div. 1963).

14 Echeverria v. Estate of Lindner, No. 018666/2002, 2005 WL 1083704, at 6 (N.Y. Super. Ct. Mar. 2, 2005).

15 Anthony J. Sebok, *supra* note 4, at 102 n.171.

16 Hall v. State, 655 A.2d 827, 830 (Del. Super. Ct. 1994).

17 Toste Farm Corp. v. Hadbury, Inc., 798 A.2d 901, 906 (R.I. 2002).

18 Johnson v. Wright, 682 N.W.2d 671, 680 (Minn. 2004).

19 "Intermeddling" can include determining trial strategy or controlling settlement.

20 Freitas v. Geddes Sav. & Loan Assn., 63 N.Y.2d 254, 261 (1984).

21 Dopp v. Yari, 927 F Supp 814 (D. N. J. 1996).

22 Anglo-Dutch Petroleum Int'l, Inc. v. Haskell, 193 S.W.3d 87 (Tex. App. 2006).

23 *Id*. at 98-99.

24 The Matter of Lynx Strategies LLC v. Ferreira, 2010 WL 2674144 (Table) (N.Y. Supp.).

25 *Id*.

26 Kelly, Grossman & Flanagan, LLP v. Quick Cash, Inc. 2012 N.Y. Slip Op. 50560(U), 7.

27 The same investment agreement that was the subject of *Echeverria* (where the funding company LawCash did not have the opportunity to brief the court on New York law) was later declared to be valid and not covered by New York's usury statutes in a suit for declaratory judgment brought by LawCash in *Plaintiff Funding Corporation d/b/a LawCash v. Echeverria.*

28 *See supra* note 2.

29 Lawsuit Fin. v. Curry, 683 N.W.2d 233, 240 (Mich. Ct. App. 2004).

30 *Id.* at 239.

31 Oasis Legal Fin. Grp., LLC v. Suthers, No. 10CV8380 (Colo. Denver Dist. Ct. Sept. 28, 2011), *available at* http://www.coloradoattorneygeneral.gov/sites/default/files/press_releases/2011/09/29/oasis_order.pdf.

32 *Id.*

33 Russell Korobkin, *Bounded Rationality, Standard Form Contracts, and Unconscionability*, 70 U. Chi. L. Rev. 1203, 1204 (2003).

34 In 2004, several members of the American Legal Finance Association entered into an agreement with the New York attorney general that requires certain best practices in legal finance transactions. Among other things, contracts with consumers must be written in the same language as the oral negotiations for English and Spanish speakers, while only the principal terms of the contract must be translated into the native language of the client for languages other than Spanish. Both Maine and Ohio have incorporated similar requirements into their legal finance statutes.

35 Jones Leasing v. Gene Phillips and Assoc., 282 S.C. 327, 318 S.E.2d 31 (Ct. App. 1984).

36 Fausone v. U.S. Claims, Inc., 915 So.2d 626 (2005).

37 *Id.* at 630.

38 *Id.*

39 Most lawsuit funding agreements, both tort and commercial, require mandatory arbitration for purposes of dispute resolution. It is important to note that the 2004 agreement with the New York attorney general, as well as the recently enacted legal finance statutes in Maine and Ohio, which were modeled after the New York agreement, all prohibit mandatory arbitration in consumer transactions with consumers in those states.

40 Buckeye Check Cashing Inc. v. Cardegna, 546 U.S. 440 (2006).

41 *Id.* at 445-446.

42 Many of these best practices are required by agreement with the New York attorney general and have been codified in Maine, Ohio and Nebraska. In addition, ALFA requires its members to adhere to similar best practices.

43 Anthony J. Sebok, *supra* note 4, at 74-94.

44 Osuna v. Albertson, 134 Cal. App. 3d 71, 82 (1982).

45 Horton v. New South Ins. Co., 468 S.E.2d 856, 858 (1996).

46 By contrast, Texas and Mississippi do allow assignment of personal injury causes of action.

47 *See* Teal E. *Luthy, Assigning Common Law Claims for Fraud*, 65 U. CHI. L. REV. 1001 (1998).

48 Sebok, *supra* note 4, at 84.

49 *Id.* at 85.

50 *See Ethics Opinions*, LAWCASH, http://www.lawcash.net/html/ethics-opinions.html.

51 Anglo-Dutch Petroleum Int'l, Inc. v. Haskell, 193 S.W.3d 87 (Tex. App. 2006).

Chapter 7

1 *See generally* LOVELL LLP, AT WHAT COST? A LOVELLS MULTI JURISDICTIONAL GUIDE TO LITIGATION COSTS (2010).

2 *See generally* C. HODGES, S. VOGENAUER & M. TULIBACKA, THE COSTS AND FUNDING OF CIVIL LITIGATION – A COMPARATIVE PERSPECTIVE, HART PUBLISHING (2010).

3 *Id.*

4 *Id.*

5 NSW LAW REFORM COMMISSION, DISCUSSION PAPER, BARRATRY MAINTENANCE AND CHAMPERTY, NO. 36, AT 7 (1994) (AUSTL.).

6 QPSX Ltd v. Ericsson Australia Pty. Ltd. (2005) 219 ALR 1 at 54 (Austl.).

7 Cambells Cash & Carry Pty Ltd. v. Fostif Pty. Ltd. (2006) 229 C.L.R. 386 (Austl.).

8 *Id.* at 88-89.

9 Brookfield Multiplex Ltd. v. Int'l Litig. Funding Partners Pte. Ltd. (2009) 180 FCR 11 (Austl.).

10 International Litigation Partners Pte. Ltd. v. Chameleon Mining NL (Receivers and Managers Appointed) (2012) HCA 45 (Austl.).

11 EXPLANATORY STATEMENT, SELECT LEGISLATIVE INSTRUMENT 2012 NO. 308, CORPORATIONS AMENDMENT REGULATION 2012 (NO. 6) AMENDMENT REGULATION 2012 (NO. 1) *available at* http://www.comlaw.gov.au/Details/F2012L02414/Explanatory%20 Statement/Text.

12 *Id.*

13 *Id.*

14 MINISTRY OF JUSTICE, PLAN FOR GROWTH: PROMOTING THE UK'S LEGAL SERVICES SECTOR 1 (2011).

15 According to the London Maritime Arbitrators Association, more maritime disputes are arbitrated in London than any other place, *available at* http://www.lmaa.org.uk/about-us-Introduction.aspx.

16 Claire Ruckin & Sofia Lind, *External Funding Booms as Litigators Plot Upturn*, LEGAL WEEK (Mar. 2008), *available at* http://www.legalweek.com/legal-week/news/1145812/external-funding-booms-litigators-plot-upturn.

17 Criminal Law Act, 1967, c. 58, § 14 (Eng.).

18 Hill v. Archbold, [1968] 1 QB 686 (Eng.).

19 *Id.* at 694-695.

20 R (Factortame Ltd.) v. Sec'y of State for Transp., [2002] EWCA (Civ) 932, [32], [2003] Q.B. 381 (Eng.).

21 Arkin v. Borchard Lines Ltd., [2005] 1 W.L.R. 3055 (Eng.).

22 *Id.* at 3069.

23 M. NAPIER, P. HURST, R. MOORHEAD, R. MUSGROVE & C. STUTT, IMPROVED ACCESS TO JUSTICE: FUNDING OPTIONS & PROPORTIONATE COSTS, THE FUTURE FUNDING OF LITIGATION – ALTERNATIVE FUNDING STRUCTURES, A SERIES OF RECOMMENDATIONS TO THE LORD CHANCELLOR, TO IMPROVE ACCESS TO JUSTICE THROUGH THE DEVELOPMENT OF IMPROVED FUNDING STRUCTURES, CIV. JUSTICE COUNCIL 53 (2007).

24 THE LAW SOCIETY, LITIGATION FUNDING, KEY ISSUES AND BACKGROUND INFORMATION 23 (2008) (ENG.).

25 Lord Justice Jackson, REVIEW OF CIVIL LITIGATION COSTS, FINAL REPORT, MINISTRY OF JUSTICE 117 (2009) (ENG.).

26 *Id.*

27 *Id.*, at 118-124.

28 ASSOCIATION OF LITIGATION FUNDERS OF ENGLAND AND WALES, CODE OF CONDUCT FOR LITIGATION FUNDERS (2011), *available at* http://www.judiciary.gov.uk/NR/rdonlyres/75D4F49E-BDC6-40BC-B379-B5A1DA82BED9/0/CodeofConductfor-LitigationFundersNovember2011.pdf.

29 *Id.* at 1-3.

30 *Id.*

31 *Id.*

Chapter 8

1 Juridica Investments Limited (UK), *About Juridica*, http://www.juridicainvestments.com.

2 Burford Group, *Theory and Practice in Litigation Risk, White Paper* (by Jonathan Molot, Chief Investment Officer) Apr. 25, 2012, at 11.

3 Kirk Hartley, *Great Example of Litigation Funding at Work*, GLOBALTORT.COM, May 2, 2012, http://www.globaltort.com/2012/05/great-example-of-litigation-funding-at-work/.

4 Briefcase Analytics, *Summary of Findings: 2012 Litigation Financing Survey*, Nov., 2012, at 5-7.

5 *Id.*

6 Juridica Investment Limited, Half year results for the six months ended 30 June 2012 at 1, http://otp.investis.com/clients/uk/juridica-investments/rns/regulatory-story.aspx?cid=319&newsid=269130.

7 BURFORD GROUP, INTERIM REPORT 2012, at 4, *available at* http://www.burfordcapital.com/wp-content/uploads/2012/10/burford_interim_2012.pdf.

8 IMF (Australia) Ltd, *2012 Full Year Results Presentation, Relating to the 2012 Annual Report*, Aug. 2012, at 9. Conversion performed on 09/24/2012, at http://www.x-rates.com/calculator/?from=EUR&to=USD&amount=1.

9 *Id.* at 7. Conversion performed on 09/24/2012, at http://www.x-rates.com/calculator/?from=EUR&to=USD&amount=1.

10 Axa and Prudential have invested in Juridica, while Fidelity has purchased a stake in Burford.

11 JURIDICA INVESTMENTS LTD., HALF YEARLY REPORT (September 17, 2012), *available at* http://otp.investis.com/clients/uk/juridica-investments/rns/regulatory-story.aspx?cid=319&newsid=269130.

12 Burford Group, supra note 7, at 1.

13 *Id.*

14 *Id.*

15 *Id.* at 3; X-Rates, Currency Calculator: Euro to US Dollar, http://www.x-rates.com/calculator/?from=EUR&to=USD&amount=1 (conversion performed on Sept. 24, 2012).

16 Execution Noble (investment company), Research Report, *Burford Capital, Uncorrelated, Superior Returns*, Aug. 18, 2010, at 5.

17 Asta Funding, Inc., Press Release, http://www.astafunding.com/releasedetail.cfm?ReleaseID=674917.

18 Esquire Bank, Products & Services, LINKEDIN.COM, http://www.linkedin.com/company/esquire-bank/products.

19 Burford Group Press Release, Dec. 12, 2011, http://www.burfordfinance.com/docs/default-document-library/burford_12de2011_rns_final.pdf.

Index

CPSIA information can be obtained
at www.ICGtesting.com
Printed in the USA
FFOW03n2241040817
38509FF

9 780988 510500